HAVE NOTHING IN YOUR HOUSES THAT YOU DO NOT KNOW TO BE USEFUL, OR BELIEVE TO BE BEAUTIFUL.

William Morris

USE *Noun:* The action of using something or the state of being used for a purpose.

ORNAMENT *Noun:* A thing used or serving to make something look more attractive but usually having no practical purpose.

USE & ORNAMENT

USE & ORNAMENT

An Exploration of the Improv Quilt

NICHOLAS BALL

For Samuel, who, like an improv quilt, was unique

Published in 2024
by Lucky Spool Media, LLC

www.luckyspool.com

5424 Sunol Blvd., Suite 10-118
Pleasanton, CA 94566
info@luckyspool.com

Text © Nicholas Ball
Editor: Bruce Darlaston
Designer: Megan McElroy
Illustrator: Ian Rawle
Rabbit and Cat Illustrations: Amelia Pease
Alice falling down rabbit hole © Laura Barrett
Styling: El Robertson, DEPTHM
Photography: Mark Robertson, DEPTHM © Lucky Spool Media, LLC
Except as follows:
Pages 3, 10, 12, 13, 29, 121, 124, 125, 128, 129,
138, 139, 147, 155, 183, 186, 192, 195, 200, 203,
211, 220, 224, 228 Nicholas Ball
Page 231 Getty Images
Page 147 Fish image Arend van den Nieuwenhiuzen
Pages 22, 23, 25 Museum Wales Collections
Pages 31, 34 Quilters' Guild Museum Collection
Pages 35, 38, 39 ,40, 41 Souls Grown Deep / Artists' Rights Society
Contributor photographs supplied and reproduced with kind permission.

9 8 7 6 5 4 3 2 1
First Edition

Printed in China

Library of Congress Cataloging-in-Publication
Data available upon request

ISBN 978-1-940655-49-9
LSID0058

CONTENTS

INTRODUCTION:
From an Attic to Ann Arbor

I wasn't supposed to be a quilter. The roadmap I sketched whilst finishing my photography degree saw me graduating art school and travelling the globe to shoot high fashion. I knew that having my work grace the cover of such magazines as 'Vogue' and 'Dazed and Confused' was a lofty ambition, yet one which I was determined to achieve. Photography was my love. I wanted to travel in the same circles as those photographers whom I so admired: Mario Testino, David LaChapelle, Gregory Crewdson. Like many of these greats, I made it to Paris, where I spent time reaping the rewards of a laidback lifestyle, none of which did anything to further the career I envisaged. Before I knew it, two years had passed and my passion for fashion had dimmed.

It's funny to think how different my life could have been if I'd been more driven and procrastinated less. My discovery of quilting after returning from France helped to bridge a creative slump. Shifting mediums was not new to me. As a child I would experiment with paints, paper, clay, and wood. I never really stuck to one thing, instead preferring to embrace a kaleidoscopic array of creativity. I believed this new exploration of quilting would follow a similar path as previous crafts, allowing for moments of expression yet never becoming anything more than a hobby. This hobby, as it was back then, began with a sewing machine purchased from a discount store, the contents of which could have just as easily sent me down a path of paper craft or beading. The fabric I sourced was of questionable quality and my adherence to the quarter inch seam was scant. Yet despite these hurdles, I was intrigued. Quilting had my attention.

Yet my love for it did not blossom from the first quilt I made. It came after a whirlwind romance of trial and error. It was improv, specifically my experiments with piecing vegetable blocks, that solidified my love, long before I knew what improvising was. In hindsight, it's strange to look back and remember a time before I appreciated spontaneity and sewing off the cuff. Everything I did at the beginning was so regimented. Patterns were followed and instructions adhered to, all within the confines of a small attic studio.

In 2014 I held aloft my Vegetable Patch quilt to an audience of fellow quilters and declared "*this quilt made me realise the quilter I want to be when I grow up*". Writing these words now, surrounded by the efforts of seven years of improvised exploration, I believe I finally have.

The journey of my quilting adolescence has been one of creative endeavour, surprise, and bitter disappointment. I have garnered knowledge through experimentation. I have been given the opportunity to share my love of improvised piecing to audiences around the world, from a handful of students in an Edinburgh village hall, to a packed conference room in Michigan. Writing 'Inspiring Improv' gave me the space to provide people with the skills to forge their own improv path and I continually delight in seeing their take on my techniques. I have learnt so much and now feel like improv quilting has always been there.

Before I took to a sewing machine and sewed my first quilt block, my exposure to the tradition of patchwork was blinkered and skewed by stereotypes. My earliest memories of quilting are not familial. There is no history of the craft in my family. No antique quilts have been passed down through the generations, and I doubt any relatives ever owned one before I began sewing and gifting them. I have the breadth and depth of American films and television shows to thank for exposing me to what I now know is just a very small part of a rich and eclectic story. Quilts that decorated sets, either draped over the back of sofas or neatly folded on beds, schooled me in believing that a quilt was only ever traditional, precise, and utilitarian.

I like to think that within quilting there exists a taxonomy of understanding. I remember conversations that would arise a decade ago when I mentioned to a friend or relative that I had taken up quilting. Their brow would furrow as they exclaimed "*you're making a quilt?*" When I replied that it was something I had always wanted to do, the response was often something along the lines of *"do you know you can buy them? Duvets, pillowcases, and everything!"*

You see, say quilt to the average Brit and they assume you're talking about a duvet: bedding filled with either natural or synthetic filling, such as down or polyester, and protected by a removable cover. To Americans, the term 'comforter' may be more familiar, though this differs from a duvet in its thickness and lack of cover. With the definition of a quilt varying depending on geographical location, you can see why some eyebrows were raised when I expressed interest in making one.

Like the richly populated animal and plant kingdoms, the taxonomy of a quilt cascades down evermore specifically. People may be aware of patchwork in the traditional sense, but the subtle differences that separate class, order, and genus are not so well known. A quilt can be pieced, either by hand or machine, but isn't always. English paper piecing and foundation paper piecing are variations on a theme. Many types of quilts, such as bargello, medallion, scrap, puff, and wholecloth exist in an overlapping Venn diagram of methods and styles.

Improv quilting has a reputation of being a penchant of the modern maker. During my years of exploration, I've encountered many quilters whose belief was that it is a new craze, born from impatience and the desire for a quick finish. Almost all are surprised to find out that examples of improvised quilts predate some of the traditionally pieced quilts they believe to be the origins of quilting.

Along with the idea that improv quilts are a product of the twenty-first century, the reasons why quilts are made and who makes them, abound with stereotypes. Traditionally born from a utilitarian need, quilts today have much more scope for meaning. They occupy a multi-faceted place in society and consciousness. As wide-ranging as the reasons for their construction are, so too are the people constructing them. No longer solely a symbol of domesticity and female pursuits, quilting spans generations and gender. Grandmothers may teach their grandsons how to quilt, but sometimes the roles are reversed.

I was a curious child. I loved museums and would collect specimens when playing in the woods or at the beach to curate my own cabinet of curiosities or 'wunderkammer'.

This thirst for knowledge continues to this day. My grandmother's house was a treasure trove of items waiting to be discovered. Whenever something unusual caught my eye, I would eagerly question her about it. Sometimes the answer was specific. "*That's a rug beater*," she might say, or of the egg slicer, "*be careful with that, the wires are sharp.*" With some of her accoutrements, their purpose was evident, yet I wanted to hear her talk about them in that long-way-around way that grandmothers do so well. Her voice was comforting and heavy with intonation. "*That*," she would explain emphatically as I queried another obscurity, "*is neither use nor ornament.*" I was obsessed with this answer and often pondered the point of a thing if it was both useless and unsightly.

My exploration of improvised quilts has shown me they exist beyond the limited realm people often assume. What constitutes an improvised quilt will vary from quilter to quilter. Many words are bandied about to describe them, with 'wonky' and 'made without thought' being some of the more frequent ones I hear. Yes, they can be spontaneous and reflective of a modernist movement, but their use and function is far from being unconsidered.

Past examples, created for the purpose of being providers of warmth, now merit elevation to works of art. The patchwork quilt, home staple and utilitarian object, can give voice to political protest; can memorialise a loved one; can be a cathartic outlet and still hold its own against art works realised in more recognised fine art media, such as paints, ceramics, and bronze. They are historical documents and family keepsakes. Whilst this book does not claim to be a complete history of improv quilts, I hope to show you that they have long existed within a duality of use and ornament, having an allure that demands further exploration.

Part One: THEN

Five and a half thousand years ago, a master carver sat at his work bench and contemplated a piece of ivory.

The task ahead was significant, for he knew what he would eventually bring forth from that ivory would be placed into the tomb of a Pharaoh of Egypt. With skilled hands he worked the raw material, carving a beardless king wearing a crown. His chisel replicated the folds and diamond pattern of a cloak, which contemporary historians think may have been quilted. This carving remained in peaceful slumber with the deceased king until 1903, when it was discovered in the Temple of Osiris at Abydos. At its new home in London's British Museum, thousands of visitors can now gaze upon what is considered to be the earliest recorded example of quilting.

Quilting has a history that spans millennia. Its existence in clothing, wall hangings, bedding, and objects of decoration has been found across the globe. There are many fine examples of silk quilts, dating from China's Eastern Zhou Dynasty. Medieval padded wear, placed under armour for comfort, is frequently mentioned in inventories of the time. In seventeenth-century Britain, quilted doublets and breeches were worn by the nobility and landed gentry. Quilts were made by women as markers of special occasions, such as weddings and births. A letter from 1811 penned by the author Jane Austen to her sister Cassandra asks *"have you remembered to collect the pieces for the patchwork?"* .

This rich repertoire of quilting reflects the many different uses and associations these objects have. Improvising has long been part of the quilt narrative. As quilting is associated with warmth and comfort, patchwork suggests a frugality and a way of using up oddments of fabric, reflective of an improvised approach. Whilst some quilts created by well-to-do women would have been made as part of a leisurely pursuit, the majority of antique quilts were practical objects. This section aims to showcase a small cross-section of quilts from three distinct periods. When thinking about which quilts to include there are many fine examples of historical improvising to consider, from a wide range of makers and places. I sought to include examples of quilting that speak to me. The inclusion of Welsh flannel quilts is to be expected since I have such an affinity with these pieces created in my homeland. Similarly, no discussion on improv quilting would be complete without mentioning those quilts which came from Gee's Bend. All the quilts showcased here evoke a similar sense of spontaneity and expressiveness associated with contemporary improvised examples. When viewed through the eyes of a twenty-first century maker, their value as works of art is clear. These are museum-worthy pieces that offer a glimpse into the lives of those who made them for far less grandiose ambitions.

WELSH QUILTS

From its source in the Cambrian Mountains, the River Teifi cuts through Mid Wales and the borders of the counties of Ceredigion, Carmarthenshire, and Pembrokeshire. It flows past the ruined abbey of Strata Florida before broadly turning. As it traverses mires and peat bogs, its choppy waters startle merlins and peregrine falcons into flight. Arcing towards the Southwest, tributaries from the rocky gorges of the valley join the rapids as they course past Tregaron, Lampeter, Llandysul, Newcastle Emlyn, and Cenarth. At Llechryd, the river begins to widen, cutting through Cilgerran gorge as it heads westward towards Cardigan. Flanked by Poppit Sands and Gwbert, the estuary finally flows into Cardigan Bay and the Teifi becomes one with the sea.

It was the water of this ancient river that helped fuel one of Wales' most important industries. The country's relationship with wool can be traced back to the pre-historic period. The rugged and wet landscape of the Welsh mountainside was a place where hardy breeds of sheep thrived, kept for their fleece and milk by diligent shepherds. For centuries after, from Anglesey to Monmouth, the importance of wool to the people of Wales continued to grow. Towns and villages saw local trade, yet it was long after the cottage industries of monastic farmers and their Middle Age spinning and weaving that the industry truly flourished. Demand for product saw wool make up for two-thirds of exports during the late seventeenth century and by the time of the industrial revolution in the early nineteenth century, the River Teifi powered dozens of mills in the surrounding valley. The ubiquitous sheep of the nearby pastures and hillsides provided fleeces that were skillfully transformed into shawls and blankets by carders, spinners, weavers, and dyers, who all flocked to the valley and the mills of the local villages. It wasn't long before wool surpassed coal as the most valuable of Wales' industries.

CALONNAU GWYRGAM
C. 19TH CENTURY

DOUBLE SIDED QUILT
1850

Dre-fach Felindre is one such village where the impact of the thriving woollen industry of the late 1800s was felt most. Owing to the swelling population, the smaller villages of Dre-fach (Small Town) and Felindre (Mill Town) merged. Cottages were erected to house the new workforce and a fresh way of living emerged from the productivity of the twenty-odd mills powered by the Teifi. With less of an importance on agriculture, life in the village was akin to the coal mining valleys of South Wales and soon shops and businesses sprang up alongside the newly built dwellings to serve the needs of the bustling community.

With the illustrious industry now over, today's residents have no use for the former mills of Dre-fach Felindre. The buildings have naturally taken on other roles, including accommodation for the many visitors the area welcomes each year. Although all standing as monuments to the past, the most important relic of that industrious bygone age is the Cambrian Mill, erected in 1902 and now home to the National Wool Museum. Both the mill and the village of Dre-fach Felindre are national heritage sites. The museum uses restored buildings and historic machinery to show visitors the journey from fleece to fabric, with hands-on opportunities for carding, spinning, and sewing along the way. As well as having a part to play in the history of the country, wool unsurprisingly weaves its way into the story of Wales' quilts too.

Historically speaking, when discussing Welsh quilts, most quilters today are familiar with the wholecloth examples. These works were meticulously hand quilted and have become the quintessential representation of Welsh quilt making. For many, it is the quilting that truly makes a Welsh quilt, rather than the piecing. Some are simple, framed designs stitched with vines, leaves, geometric shapes, and echo quilting. Other makers proved more ambitious, with one example in the collection of the National Museum Wales showcasing emblems of Welshness, including leeks, daffodils, and dragons.

Quilts of the past were commonly born out of necessity, rather than artistic vision. Welsh wholecloth quilts were often double sided, so that they could be rotated and their use prolonged. Once age and wear began to show, old quilts were repurposed, becoming the wadding for newer ones. Torn pieces were cut and sewn into new patchwork. Though not as well-known, it is these examples of pieced Welsh quilts that echo the spontaneity of today's improvised quilts.

It is no surprise that woollen fabrics found their way into many of these early pieced quilts. When a blanket no longer served its purpose, it was reimagined into a new patchwork quilt, often featuring bold stripes, bars, and centre medallions.

It is these quilts that evoke memories of early American patchwork, particularly examples produced by Amish communities, which share a similar graphic quality. There are Welsh quilts that pre-date some Amish examples and it has been debated that immigration patterns led to an interaction of Welsh and American quilters in the nineteenth century, resulting in a design influence. Quilt historian Dorothy Osler's, 'Amish Quilts and the Welsh Connection' is an important and authoritative work which examines the common features of both and presents evidence to suggest a strong creative connection.

With so many mills producing wool, Welsh quilts from the Teifi Valley were wholly homemade and the only truly indigenous examples. Local wool was not only used to make the fabric for the quilt top, but also provided the filling in the form of a worn-out blanket or bits of sheep's fleece picked from the hedgerows. Some of the mills were known to have a quilter working in the loft above, using the abundant flannel leftovers and the raw product for batting.

There are examples of tailors' quilts, serving as a showcase for the many varieties of wool produced by a mill. I like to imagine that woollen offcuts found their way into nearby homes, and were lovingly pieced into quilts by the wives of the mill workers. A scrap may have been sewn into a flying geese unit, another perhaps forming the corner stone of the quilt. It wasn't just women at this time who were producing improvised quilts. The National Museum Collection houses many fine examples of quilts pieced by tailors working during the latter part of the nineteenth century.

I have an indirect connection to one such tailor who, whilst there is no evidence he ever made a quilt, would have almost certainly used wool in his trade. Born in 1815 in Dihewyd, Ceredigion, John Harris is the third great grandfather of my partner Barry and was known as 'Teilwr Bach Dihewyd' (Dihewyd's Little Tailor). At three foot, eight inches, his diminutive stature made him a local curiosity and children would follow him around whenever his work took him to their village. His wife Margaret was taller at five foot, five inches. Together the pair had nine children, with eight reaching adulthood.

JOHN HARRIS
DIHEWYD'S LITTLE TAILOR

John was rumoured to have refused calls from showmen to join the circus and instead made tours through various counties accompanied by his family. Quite the celebrity, he invited people to send six pence to his address to receive his photograph. Though a jovial man, he didn't take kindly to people mocking his height. Once, during a country fair, a drover warned him that if he wasn't quiet, he'd put him in his pocket, to which Teilwr Bach indignantly replied, "*then there would be more sense in your pocket than has ever been in your head!*" According to local lore, John liked to frequent the village pub. It was said that he would become so intoxicated, Margaret would carry him home in her apron. Teilwr Bach died in 1893 and was buried in the churchyard at Eglwys Llanwyddalis, Dihewyd.

With the introduction of cotton and more luxurious imported fabrics such as silks and chintz, Welsh quilt makers became exposed to more colours and patterns. Sateen and paisley prints found their way into quilt tops, which were pieced in a liberated way using tiny pieces and fine colour combinations. Many of these quilts, owing to their utilitarian nature, endured a similar fate to their woollen counterparts and were often discarded due to wear. If they were kept, for reasons of sentimentality, they were poorly stored in damp homes.

TARIAN Y GWEITHIWR
TEILWR BACH'S OBITUARY
THURSDAY, JANUARY 26, 1893

...rian y Gweithiwr

COFNODYDD GWLADOL A GWEITHFAOL.

(REGISTERED FOR TRANSMISSION ABROAD.)

DYDD IAU, IONAWR 26, 1893.

Pris Ce...

William Price, Cyfarthfa; Daniel Jones, George Pit; Thomas Lewis, Aberaman; William Phelps, Graig, Gadlys; a Morgan Williams, Werfa.

Dymunir ar yr etholedigion hyn i anfon eu cyhoeddiadau yn llawn i'r Ysgrifenydd mor gynted ag y byddo modd.

D. PARKER, Ysg.

AT LOWEN Y GLO CARBO.

Bydded hysbys i chwi y cynnelir cyfarfod nesaf y Dosbarth dydd Sadwrn nesaf, Ton Slain, yn y lle arferol yn Brynaman.

Fel y gwyddoch, y mae yn arferiad i'r glowyr i gael eu glo tai am tua hanner y pris, ond fod hynny yn gwahaniaethu mewn rhai glofeydd. Y mae dymuniad ar i bob cynrychiolydd i ddyfod a'r dull a'r pris y maent yn cael eu glo tai i'r cyfarfod dydd Sadwrn nesaf. Bydd hynny yn fantais, heblaw i'r rhai sydd mewn helbul yn ei gylch yn bresenol.

Hefyd dymunir cael eich barn ar y cwestiynau sydd dan sylw y Dosbarth oddiar y cyfarfod diweddaf, sef y dull o ddal cyfreithiwr y Dosbarth yn y dyfodol. Yn ail, a ydym fel Dosbarth yn ffurfio trysorfa neu rhyw beth cyffelyb i gynorthwyo gweddwon glowyr mewn amgylchiadau o golli eu gwyr mewn damweiniau, sef un yn unigol yn cael ei ddiwedd. Cychwynodd y syniad yma ar gôn fod y wlad yn gyffredinol yn teimlo ac yn cydran at weddwon ac amddifaid ar ol damweiniau mawrion lle collir llawer o fywydau fel y dygwyddodd y Parc Slip, ond lle collir un neu ddau o fywydau nad oes teimlad cyffelyb yn cael ei arddangos, er ei fod yn gymaint o golled i'r un hyny golli ei gwr ac i'r rhai hyny a gollasant eu gwyr mewn damweiniau mawrion, ond nad oedd yr un teimladau yn cael ei ddangos. Rhywbeth tebyg i hyny oedd y syniad, ac i'r cyfeiriad hwn y caron gael eich barn, a oes modd i wneud rhywbeth, a hyny mewn modd y bydd heddwch yn ei ganlyn wrth geisio gweinyddu cyfiawnder.

Fod chwe cheiniog o lawy i ddyfod i'r cyfarfod dydd Sadwrn nesaf i gynorthwyo gweithwyr Car Bryn ac Abercrave Junction am yr amser y buont yn segur yn herwydd methu cael eu talu. Mae Mr Abraham wedi addaw dyfod i'r cyfarfod dydd Sadwrn.

ENOCH RHYS.

DIENYDDIAD HYNOD YN GLASGOW.

Yn Glasgow, bore dydd Mercher diweddaf, dienyddiwyd y dyn William McKeown, yr hwn a lofruddiodd y fenyw Elizabeth Conorin, yn West Lodge, Renfrewshire. Glasgow Herald Her can...

MARWOLAETH Y TEILWR BACH.

Yr ydym yn cael o Sir Aberteifi fod John Harris, Ffestfonen, yr hwn a adnabyddid wrth yr enw Teilwr Bach, ddiweddar, wedi marw yn 78 oed. Nid oedd ond 3 troedfedd ac 8½ modfedd o daldra, ac yn pwyso rhyw 66 pwys, tra yr oedd ei wraig yn fenyw dal ac yn pwyso 196 pwys. Yr oedd ganddo naw o blant—wyth o ba rai sydd yn awr yn fyw, ac yn bersonau o faintioli da.

CORFF YN NGWEITHIAU DWFR ABERDAR.

Bore dydd Gwener deuwyd o hyd i gorff marw dyn yn Ngweithian Dwfr Aberdar. Yr oedd ei goesau wedi eu cylymu a rhaff. Adnabyddwyd y corff fel eiddo un Walter Jones, labrwr, 18, Elizabeth Street, Aberdar, yr hwn a letyai gyda'i chwaer, ac a gollwyd er y Sul o Tachwedd, a chredir ei fod wedi bod yn y dwfr a ysir gan ran fawr o'r trigolion am yn agos i saith wythnos.

DAMWAIN LOFAOL DDYCHRYNLLYD.

SAITH O FYWYDAU WEDI EU COLLI.

Dydd Llun diweddaf, yn y pwll newydd a suddir yn Aberdare Junction gan gwmni Dowlais, cymerodd damwain angeuol ofidus iawn le, trwy yr hon y collwyd saith o fywydau, ac yr archollwyd tri o bersonau eraill. Y mae y pwll yn awr 260 o lathenni o ddyfnder, yr hwn sydd wedi cael ei walio oll o fewn 20 troedfedd i'r gwaelod. Rhoddwyd pob gwaith heibio bore dydd Llun er i ymchwiliad gael ei wneud ar y lle, a chyhoeddwyd yr oll yn ddiogel a boddhaol. Am ddau o'r gloch yn y prydnawn, aeth 27 o sincwyr at eu gwaith, dan arweiniad Griffith Wood. Aeth pob peth yn mlaen yn rhagorol hyd yohydig wedi chwech o'r gloch, pryd y cyffrowyd rhai o'r dynion gan gwymp o'r oehr, ac yn mhen ennyd arall daeth careg fawr, yn pwyso o saith i wyth tynell, ar y gweithwyr, yr hwn i laddodd chwech o honynt yn y man, gan anafu eraill. Rhoddwyd yr alarwm, a daeth cynorthwy buan o ben y pwll, ac ar unwaith, dechreuwyd codi y meirw. Yr oedd rhai o'r cyrff wedi eu niweidio i'r fath raddau, fel y gorfodid eu cario i'w cartref mewn sachau. Bu farw y seithfed, Richard Davies, yn fuan wedi iddo gyrhaedd pen y pwll. Enwau y lladdedigion ydynt,—
Henry Caddy, 36 oed, Graigwen road, Pontypridd, yn briod.
Robert Roberts, 29 oed, Margaret Street, Navigation, dyn sengl.
Cadwalader Williams, 25 oed, Margaret...

A proponent of the salvaging and restoration of antique Welsh quilts is Jen Jones. Jen is the founder of The Welsh Quilt Centre in Lampeter, a market town in the county of Ceredigion, and an expert on Welsh quilts. It is through her knowledge and passion that I have come to further understand the rich history of quilting in Wales.

After her marriage to a Welshman, Jen came to live in Wales in 1971. In America, quilts were part of her upbringing. She describes them as "*a cherished part of everyone's heritage*", yet she was unaware of the tradition of quilting in Wales before her arrival. In her book 'Welsh Quilts', Jen recalls the moment she became involved with them, calling it a "*salvage operation*". Her first encounter was at a local auction. Mixed in one of the bundles of linen, kicking around on the floor, was a beautifully stitched floral wholecloth.

Jen bought the bundle for one pound, leading to a "*surprise beginning*". Jen's obsession with collecting Welsh quilts and textiles has now spanned over forty years and her perseverance has been integral in helping to preserve this important part of Wales' heritage. As Jen's collection grew, the need for a permanent location to house it became apparent.

"*Having acquired a vast private collection, hopefully representing the whole spectrum of Welsh quilts, we were invited to venues worldwide, but knew they needed a permanent home. The old Lampeter Town Hall came available; it was falling to bits and needed saving, a fortunate coincidence.*"

The Welsh Quilt Centre is a remarkable venue. Officially opened in 2010 by King Charles III and Queen Camilla, then His Royal Highness, The Prince of Wales and The Duchess of Cornwall, I first visited in 2016 during the Unforgettable exhibition and saw many bold and striking examples of nineteenth century Welsh flannel quilts. These were displayed alongside quintessential items of Welshness, including hats and traditional costumes. It was through viewing these quilts that I came to appreciate how a working tradition and object of use could at the same time be a beautiful piece of art.

The provenance of these objects often tells a different story. Unlike today, the makers of such quilts would not have placed any great emphasis on the longevity and preservation of their work. As well as taking on a secondary use, such as covering a sick animal, early quilts that had reached the end of their life, either through use or neglect, were often cut up, re-sewn, and adapted to new purpose as part of another quilt. Jen occasionally encounters quilts which have been re-backed or added to. Many were re-covered, though sometimes not very sympathetically. In my talks with Jen, I've learnt of some of the more unusual places she's rescued pieces from.

"As quilts were part of household bedding, they were not always treated with respect. I found a really wonderful geometric flannel quilt in a bag of discarded linen in a farm outbuilding just outside Llandeilo. Another gem, from Llanrhystud, was between a mattress and the box springs (protecting the new mattress of course). Another stunner was covering an old 'Fergie' in a barn."

Jen has curated a rich and varied collection, with many fine examples of pieced and wholecloth quilts. Quite a number can be seen to use random leftovers from drapers and tailors of the times. I've spoken to Jen at length about my love of improvised piecing and was pleased to hear that she shares this passion. Though not a quilter, she would prefer to adopt a freer approach if she were to begin quilt making. When looking at her collection, it is the *"wonderful unexpected designs of the flannel patchworks, totally lacking in the precision of most of the "better" wholecloth quilts"* that she believes best embraces this liberated, less structured approach.

It is evident that Welsh quilt-makers have produced some of the best examples of early quilts. Despite the wholecloth being most associated with the country, it is the pieced flannel quilts which best show a liberated style of improvised quilting. At the time of their construction, these quilts were meant to be used. The fact that they survive to be viewed by contemporary audiences is a rare thing. A huge debt of gratitude is owed to people like Jen, who through dedication and hard work have elevated these wonders of Welsh history from simple bedding to museum-worthy objects.

CRAZY QUILTS

Before Queen Victoria ascended the British throne in 1837, the social and economic effects of the Industrial Revolution were already being widely felt, not only in the monarch's own country, but across the continent and the world. Manufacture and transport had been transformed by steam and industry was king. Cities swelled, along with the coffers of the nouveau riche. As a result of this new way of life, homes of the middle and upper-classes were exquisitely detailed. Rooms were full of ornamentation: carved wooden furniture, paintings, rugs, window dressings, and many, many knick-knacks. Ostentatious embellishment was applied to everything. If one were to travel back in time, amongst the many accoutrements of the Victorian home, a crazy quilt in the parlour would be a common sight. Also called 'slumber robes' or 'couch throws', these textile pieces were a departure from traditional quilts and showcase irregular compositions, rather than an established, geometric pattern. Rich crimsons, golds, and teals collide in a riotous explosion of colour and texture.

The fractured look of crazy quilts was in part inspired by the highlighting of Japanese ceramics during the Centennial Exposition of 1876 in Philadelphia, Pennsylvania, and were born after the nineteenth century's booming textile industry. Increased trade saw more exotic fabrics reach the homes of middle-class women, who took to patchwork not for reasons of practicality, but as a display of wealth. They were not only cash rich, but also had the leisure time to sit and stitch for the many hours that these types of quilt demanded, whilst servants took care of the household. The quilts they produced were their Victorian take on international design and women became truly enraptured by them. An anonymous poem printed in 'Good Housekeeping' in 1890 alluded to this with the words:

Oh, the crazy-quilt mania triumphantly raves,
And maid, wife, and widow are bound as its slaves

Crazy quilts suffer from an identity crisis. The vast majority were made from two layers: an elaborate top of hundreds of individual pieces and a fabric foundation. A lack of wadding and the stitches that bind the layers together make 'crazy patchwork' a more accurate description. Despite this, crazy quilts deserve a closer look when exploring improvisation.

QUILT TOP
C. 1885

Their makers were free to combine silk, velvet, chenille, bouclé, and brocade in unique and expressive ways. Non-traditional piecing showcased the maker's skill, ingenuity, and flare for design. These quilts are imbued with personality that reflects the liberated approach today's improvisers adopt.

With form being less of a consideration, makers were free to use smaller, more irregular pieces, often incorporating oddments of high-society fashion fabrics, ribbons, and heirloom lace.

Cigarette manufacturers took advantage of the desire for silk by including small printed pieces in their packaging, which were enthusiastically collected like the trading cards of today.

As well as their eclectic array of fabrics, crazy quilts are distinguished for their use of meticulous embroidery, inspired by English needlework, which appears atop the patchwork seams in a variety of lavish threads. A great number of decorative stitches were used, with publications of the day feeding the appetite of sewers with new and exciting designs which could be transferred onto the fabric. Alongside more common stitches, such as feather stitch, chevron stitch, and chain stitch, more intricate designs, influenced by nature and the exoticism of Asia, were common. Insects were popular, with spiders thought to bring luck to the maker. Family events and meaningful verses were often also stitched onto the patchwork. Everything was done to excess, with makers embellishing the embellished. Some examples serve as memory quilts and evidence items of clothing in their construction, often accompanied by an embroidered name and date.

After the heyday of the craze during the late 1800s, the appeal of crazy quilts trickled down through the classes to reach women in more rural areas. The worn clothing of the more affluent was often repurposed for patchwork and less expensive packs of silk scraps could be purchased from mills. Those living more domesticated lives often replaced luxurious fabrics with more readily available working cloths, like sturdy flannel and cotton, and did away with the ornate stitching. By the Edwardian era, tastes became more restrained and crazy quilting fell out of fashion, having grown in popularity, peaked, and faded from favour all in the span of a quarter century.

IRISH CRAZY PATCHWORK COVERLET
C. 1880

GEE'S BEND QUILTS

This story too starts with a river, or more specifically, a horseshoe bend of the Alabama that encompasses the small, isolated hamlet of Boykin, better known as Gee's Bend. Located along the Black Belt of Alabama State, named first for the dark, fertile topsoil ubiquitous to the region, Gee's Bend's history is one rooted in slavery. The area had all the desirable qualities for cotton production, and in 1816 Joseph Gee bought a fifteen-mile stretch of land and established a plantation, worked by enslaved African Americans. Many of today's residents have a direct ancestry to the slaves of the Pettway Plantation, established in 1845 by Mark Pettway. After the end of the Civil War, many former slaves remained, working as sharecroppers and establishing an all-black community.

Despite their emancipation, the community of Gee's bend continued to face hardships during the Reconstruction era. Income was dependent on the harvest. Many residents were indebted not only to landowners for rent on their poorly insulated cabins, which lacked electricity and running water, but also to neighbouring businessmen for seeds and fertiliser. During the Roosevelt presidency, an investigation into the conditions of farming communities highlighted their plight. In 1937, as part of the New Deal, the government purchased the land, subdivided it amongst the residents, and took steps towards improvement. A school was established, along with a general store and a blacksmith. During this period, photographs taken to document the lives of the people of Gee's Bend showed women making quilts. Their cabins were filled with them; they covered beds, the floors, and the walls. Like many, the women quilted for warmth. The culture they were raised in emphasised sustainability, so they used scraps of whatever fabric they had to hand, including aprons, cornmeal sacks, and worn denim.

The ethos of improv quilting is perfectly summed up by one Gee's Bend quilter, Mensie Lee Pettway, who said, "*Ought not two quilts ever be the same*". With their rural isolation directly affecting their access to materials, the quilts produced by the residents of Gee's Bend are testament to this and have a deep sense of place.

PIG IN A PEN
MINNIE SUE COLEMAN
C. 1970

Though quilt-making had been a cultural tradition in the community for generations, the work of the Gee's Bend quilters saw wider recognition during the 1960s. With the Civil Rights Movement gaining momentum, the Freedom Quilting Bee was established by Episcopalian priest Francis X. Walter to improve the socioeconomic status of rural African Americans. Quilt makers were able to generate income by selling their work to outsiders through auctions held in New York City. The resulting revenue allowed the women of Gee's Bend to better-equip their homes and support their families. In 1967, Gee's Bend was visited by Lee Krasner, wife of Jackson Pollock, who purchased three quilts for the home she shared with her husband. During the 1980s, art collector William Arnett took an interest in the work of undiscovered African American artists across nine Southeastern US states. In 2010 he founded the Souls Grown Deep Foundation, dedicated to documenting, preserving, and promoting the work of African American artists. The Gee's Bend quilters are amongst more than 160 artists represented and the profile of these quilts has continued to be elevated through exhibitions at prestigious establishments such as the Museum of Fine Arts in Houston, the Whitney Museum, The Philadelphia Museum of Art, and the Smithsonian Institute. In 2006, the US postal service issued a set of commemorative stamps that showcased the quilts' bold designs and vibrant use of colour. This exposure helped solidify the quilts of Gee's Bend's deserved place in the lexicon of not only fellow quilters, but American art.

Taught by their grandmothers, mothers, and aunts, Gee's Bend's women of today continue a tradition whose origins lie in survival. Yet despite an article by the 'New York Times' describing their ancestors' quilts, as "*some of the most miraculous works of modern art America has produced*" many residents have expressed that the acclaim earned has not resulted in economic advancement. Many continue to live in poverty, limiting their ability to connect to a wider audience. In February 2021, in partnership with Souls Grown Deep and Nest, a non-profit organisation dedicated to supporting the responsible growth and creative engagement of the hand-worker, the e-commerce site Etsy began selling Gee's Bend quilts online, covering fees for a period of time and providing social equity and economic opportunity to the community. Donations to support the Gee's Bend community through the Souls Grown Deep Foundation go towards providing free computer and internet access, training for quilters in business strategy, and regular fine art studio photography of the quilts, all with the hope of laying the groundwork for future sustainability.

BLOCKS AND STRIPS AND STRINGS
MARY LEE BENDOLPH
C. 2002

BLOCKS
LORETTA PETTWAY
C. 2002

The American fashion designer Greg Lauren has celebrated the work of the Gee's Bend quilters through Mosaic, a recent collaboration with fourteen quilters living in the hamlet today. The designer admits to having a great love for quilts and the handmade. He worked with the women to create a collection of ninety-six garments, including bomber jackets, parkas, and wrap dresses, all of which reflect the bold and geometric simplicity of their quilts. These expressive and colourful pieces of clothing were created from panels sewn by hand by the Gee's Benders, using scraps from Lauren's atelier. The lining of each piece features a biography of the quilter and their signature is handwritten on the outside.

HOUSETOP
MARY LEE BENNETT
C. 1965

Lauren is committed to reusing pre-loved textiles and often challenges archetypes through his choice of materials. This collaboration serves to not only elevate an under-acknowledged community of quilters whose work is often relegated to craft, but also echos the make-do ethos of Gee's Bend. The quilters were compensated for their labour and all profits from the sale of the pieces were put back directly into the community. The collection was displayed at Bergdorf Goodman's Men's Store on Fifth Avenue in New York City, placing the quilters right at the crossroad of high fashion.

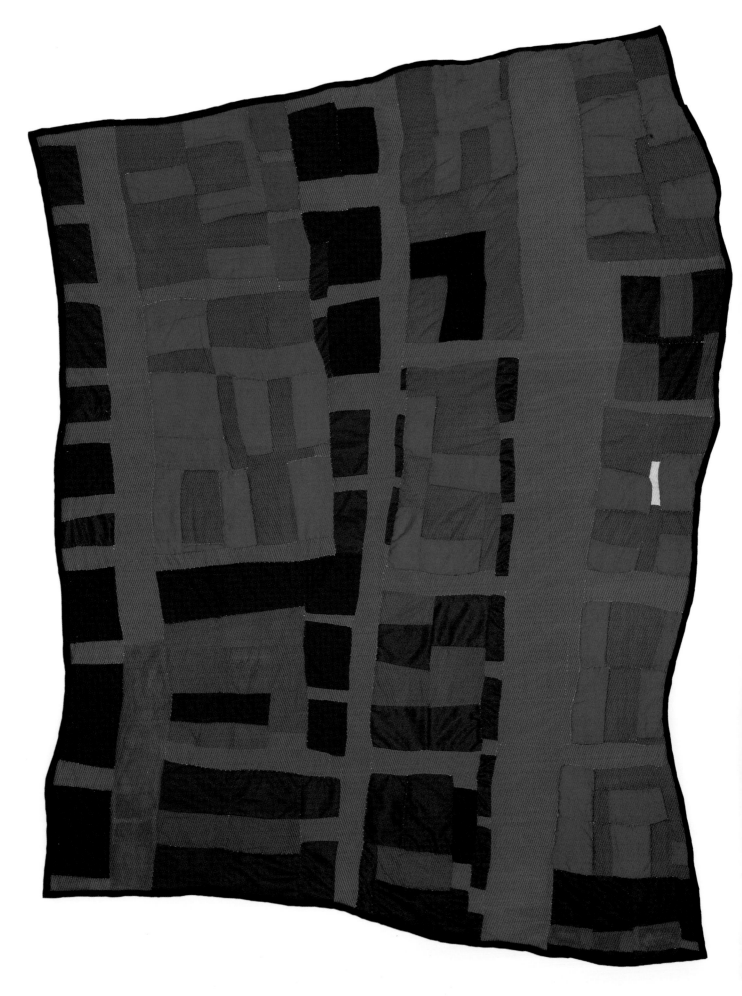

For three generations, the women of Gee's Bend have stitched together fabrics in unprescribed ways, creating hundreds of masterpieces that have instilled a sense of artistic freedom in countless quilters since. Few in today's modern quilting movement have not been wholly inspired by the legacy of these groundbreaking and influential works. Though the quilts that have come out of Gee's Bend are in no doubt a significant contribution to the oeuvre of improvised quilting, more important are the women who made them. Annie Mae Young, Mini Sue Coleman, Loretta Pettway, Lucy Mingo, Lucy T. Pettway, and dozens of others; these quilters stitched their struggles into each seam. Their quilts are stories of deprivation, racism, and resilience. Through organisations like Souls Grown Deep, the Gee's Bend quilters elaborate on these stories in their own words, their own voices, and I have been deeply moved by their frank and honest accounts.

In the winter of 1965, the Gee's Bend community was visited by Martin Luther King, who addressed the watching crowd with the words *"you are somebody"* through a torrential downpour. It feels right that this message be spoken ever-louder today to recognise these amazing women, whose creative talents abounded and continue to abound, despite the repressive circumstances of their lives.

BLOCKS AND STRIPS
IRENE WILLIAMS
C. 2003

Part Two: **NOW**

Despite the centuries that have passed since the construction of the earliest quilts, the fundamental nature of what constitutes this beloved object has not changed. A quilt is most often defined as 'multi-layered textile', traditionally composed of three layers: a woven top, a layer of wadding, and a woven back. None of the historical examples we have explored shy too far away from this accepted definition and are, at their core, fabric and thread. The same is true of quilts made today. Blocks or units are pieced, or perhaps a wholecloth approach is adopted, the top is basted and the layers are secured with stitching. It is this meditative process that links us to our quilting ancestors and is the art of quilt making at its most basic.

What has changed is the quilt's intended use and the types of people making them. We have already learnt from evaluating past quilts that there was a definite focus on function rather than form. As a contemporary maker, I often contemplate what thoughts drifted through the minds of past quilters as they stitched. Would this crib quilt be warm enough to see an infant through winter? Will this quilting work provide enough income to feed my family? The quilts were born out of necessity, rather than creativity.

Quilts made today cannot be so easily pigeon-holed. The reasons for making a quilt vary tremendously. They continue to move beyond being simply providers of warmth and their definition of utility is much broader. For today's quilters, social media is the twenty-first century equivalent of the quilting bee. Despite the consuming nature of the various platforms and interfaces with which we interact daily, this new normal brings the words, and work, of countless other creatives right to our fingertips. I have connected with hundreds of quilters whose work has inspired and informed. Both on and offline, quilters and sewers participate in bees, block swaps, and retreats, fostering a community that is bursting with inspiring makers.

This section will introduce eleven contemporary quilters whose work challenges what the function of a quilt should be. There are of course countless makers working in the improv style, and to showcase them all in one book would be quite an undertaking. The following therefore is a snapshot of quilters with whom I have connected, either through social media, in-person events, or simply from having a deep admiration of their work. Some may be familiar to you, whilst others you may be discovering for the first time. I believe all are inspiring and the eclectic array of work that follows, highlights the many ways to make an improv quilt in a contemporary setting.

JO AVERY

LINLITHGOW, SCOTLAND

My memory works best to recall moments of import or significance. Ask me what I ate last week and I would struggle to answer, yet like those people who know exactly where they were when Apollo 11 touched down on the Moon, I remember the moment I first meet Jo Avery as if it were yesterday. In 2014, stepping out of a London hotel lift, I saw a face I recognised from Instagram. This encounter was not that surprising, since around the corner from the hotel a quilting retreat was in full swing. It was the first I'd attended and a chance for me to meet some members of the online quilting community in person. Jo smiled as she recognised me too and since then, though many of the other faces I saw that weekend have long since faded from memory, she and I have remained friends.

Jo has been playing with fabric and yarn for as long as she can remember. In the 1990s, inspired by the silk remnants she received from a dressmaker friend, her love affair with improvised piecing began, though at the time, similar to my initial foray into the technique, she was unaware she was practicing improv.

"I had no idea that's what it was called. I used to sew the remnants together into giant panels and then sell them back to her to make into one-off patchwork ball gowns. The remnants were all sorts of different shapes and sizes, including curves, which I fitted and pieced together. I would now call this 'scrappy improv' and it was an incredibly useful training ground for me as far as patchwork construction was concerned, but at the time I had no idea what I was doing, I just made it up as I went along!"

40 LAYERS OF QUILTING
2019

Jo's journey into improvised piecing resonates with my own. When I sewed my first vegetable patch block, I too had a similar feeling of the unknown. Since those silk scraps, Jo now clearly has a firm understanding of improvised techniques, aided in part by the influential contemporary makers she has encountered along the way. A lecture she attended by Nancy Crow "*changed her life*" and confirmed the idea that quilting was an art form.

"Nancy's approach changed my thinking and I was blown away by her quilts. She was so ahead of her time and I feel a lot of modern quilting is just catching up now with what she was doing in the 1980s."

Much of Jo's work is informed by her natural affinity for colour. It was this expressive use of colour that first attracted me to Jo's quilts. We share a love of saturated tones and are drawn to similar palettes. We all know that colour choice is subjective and how to choose them for quilt making is a question I get asked a lot. I often talk to quilters who struggle to move beyond their comfort zone and find themselves using the same colours again and again. Jo, who has delivered many lectures on colour theory for quilters, believes there is a comfortableness in the familiar.

"I don't think there is anything wrong with familiar colour choices. We all have a set of colours that we are drawn to and love using. Students who came to my classes would often choose fabrics that exactly matched their outfit and I don't believe using your favourite colours over and over again to be wrong. Whenever I try to take myself too far away from my colour comfort zone, I am always disappointed. My favourite pieces are those made with all the colours that I love. Luckily for me, I like a lot of colours! My advice would be to concentrate on tone as much as colour. You can use all sorts of colours together harmoniously, as long as they are the same tone."

For her quilts, Jo combines pinks, greens, and teals to create detailed pieces that evoke a sense of whimsy. Her compositions are playgrounds, inviting the viewer's eye across the surface to explore all the intricate details. Her love of hand techniques, such as needle-turn appliqué and embroidery, allows her to embrace both modern and traditional quilting aesthetics, with the resulting work still being quintessentially Jo. She uses varying thread weights to great effect, often combining hand and machine quilting. With three Aurifil® thread collections to her name, she clearly enjoys experimenting with texture. I asked Jo if the slow and steady method of hand quilting gives her a greater connection to the work, compared to a machine quilted piece. Though more of a connection was not always the case, she nevertheless embraces the technique with gusto.

DANDELION CLOCKS
2019

"I love to hand stitch and would do it all day long if my hands were up to it. It is so soothing and satisfying to me and never feels like work (which using the machine sometimes does). I also like the texture you can achieve with hand quilting; it gives a richness and depth to the finished piece."

In Jo's pieces there is a place for even the smallest scrap. Her charming mini houses, with their tiny windows and doors, are immensely inspiring and I've long wanted to combine them with one of my own triangle colour studies to create a hillside village. Some months ago, I drew a little sketch to visualise how such a collaboration would look. As improv piecing can be such a spontaneous process, I wondered if Jo was a planner. How do her quilts begin? I'm always intrigued to hear if people go in with a firm concept of the finished quilt or whether they just see where the sewing takes them, two approaches which my own process often bridges.

"I always start with an idea, usually something that I'm drawn to and that I find aesthetically pleasing. It could be something in nature, a piece of art, or another quilt. Ideas often come to me on walks or in the shower and I will jot them down in my day book, perhaps with a thumbnail sketch. As I dabble in many different styles and crafts, I then need to work out how best to reinterpret whatever has caught my eye — would it work best as a modern abstract quilt, a needle-turn appliqué pattern, or even an embroidery? I will spend a good while mulling this over in the background, visualising different approaches and planning what I want to do."

I wasn't surprised to learn of the inspiration Jo takes from the world around her. Her love of nature is evident in her dandelion clock quilts and bird appliqués. Many of her quilts feature petals and leaf tendrils, and showcase her wonderful use of freehand curves. Once the idea is formed, Jo takes it to paper.

"If I decide on a quilt, then I will make a quick pencil sketch to fix the idea and then start pulling fabric. Once I begin piecing, I work very quickly, having previously done a lot of the thinking and decision making in my head."

Looking at Jo's oeuvre, it's clear to see that she approaches quilt making with a full arsenal. As someone who rarely combines different techniques in a single quilt, I applaud this more-is-more approach, which makes Jo's quilts joyous objects that demand detailed exploration.

"I have a problem with adding more and more details. I need to learn to leave more open space and not keep cramming in content. I am not a 'less-is-more' sort of person and cannot manage any sort of minimalism, but I have to be careful not to go over the top with my maximalism! Getting the balance right is so important and something I am still practicing."

JOURNEY TO THE CENTRE OF A FLOWER
2021

RUSSELL BARRATT

LONDON, ENGLAND

As a self-taught textile artist, Russell Barratt likes to leave certain things to chance. This is evident in his bold and joyful quilts. A piece that he'd imagined would be small can grow into something much larger. More stitching or appliqué is added to long-finished wall hangings. His signature polka dots, used as a unifier, are a familiar yet never regimented sight. Sometimes he adds, whilst at other times the idea of chance means cutting bits away. Like all improvisers, he fully embraces the unintended.

With a background in fashion and costume design, Russell's exploration of improvised quilting began purely as a way of displaying some of his favourite fabric scraps. He now repurposes used clothing and found objects to wonderful effect. Russell is one of the more recent improv quilters I have had the pleasure of encountering through my social media scrolling. It was a delightfully quirky quilt which first caught my attention, featuring bold diagonal stripes, paint-stained gingham, appliquéd dots, and a Kylie Minogue tee shirt. I was familiar with the use of this clothing staple as a way to make quilts, yet have always assumed them to have been cut up and pieced together. Russell had used the Kylie tee shirt whole, featuring front and not-quite-centre in his composition.

LUCKY, LUCKY, LUCKY
2021

Russell's use of clothing is commendable, not only because of the wonderful pieces he creates, but also because of the sustainable use of the fabric. Previously loved yet no longer worn tee shirts, whole shirts, complete with collars and buttonhole placket, sports socks, and a vintage dress are just a few of the items that have found themselves reimagined. A late 2021 finish, As Old As My Tongue And A Little Bit Older Than My Teeth (named after a saying his maternal grandmother used in response to the question of her age) features a worn shift dress and kitsch tea towels. The dress was an eBay find and Russell was warned by the seller that it was damaged, yet that did not dissuade him. Recycling is key to his practice and the resulting quilts are rich in narrative thanks to the raw materials.

"All the fabrics I use are secondhand or pre-loved. I've been known to re-use thread where possible. There's nothing I love more than a trip to a charity shop in search of quilting treasure! People often send me their old clothes to use. I've even used things I've found in the street. There's so much potential with used fabrics, it doesn't really make sense to me not to use what already exists."

As well as clothing, Russell has a passion for domestic materials: bed sheets, linens, and tea towels, which he uses frequently in his work as *"they inspire memories of my formative years, helping my mum with chores and the precise way of doing them."* When asked where else his inspiration comes from, Russel has a commonality with other improv quilters in his acknowledgement of the quilts of Gee's Bend. It was after seeing a book on the collective works that he began to make sense of what he was doing and feels we all *"owe a huge debt to the Gee's Bend quilts."*

SELF PORTRAIT
2021

Many of Russell's earlier pieces began life as wall-hangings. He would layer clothing and fabric offcuts, yet never intended to quilt them. This assembling of layers is a practice he continues today when working on new pieces.

"In between making quilts I continually work on little embroideries and samples, a few scraps sewn together. Then when I've got some I like, I lie them flat and start adding and removing other fabrics and things until I've got something that appeals to me. Often, it's during this process that a narrative comes into my mind. Combining something with a completely different shape, pattern, or clashing colour usually delivers a satisfying result."

**AS OLD AS MY TONGUE AND A LITTLE
BIT OLDER THAN MY TEETH**
2021

JEN BROEMEL

INDIANAPOLIS, INDIANA, USA

Jen Broemel worked as an architect in Indianapolis until her third child was born, after which she began to focus on her studio practice. She describes the results of this practice as "*vibrantly coloured, geometrically abstracted paintings with cloth and thread*". She has a love of experimentation that is evident in her eclectic pieces, which artfully showcase fabric manipulation and a passion for "*putting together and cutting apart, constructing and reconstructing; a cycle that…symbolises the happenstance of life*". Like many quilters, Jen is drawn to the tactility of cloth. Through her creative process, she is captivated by the layering of materials and "*the way the overlapping coats of coloured cloth and thread mix and blend, transforming and guiding the work, adding texture, contrast, and comfort with every stitch.*"

I first learnt of Jen and her work when she approached me to be part of The Art of Improv: a series of interviews with visual artists about working in the improvised style. I was honoured to be featured and grateful for the inspiration I found, not only directly through Jen's own work, but also the multidisciplinary mix of makers the project introduced me to. As well as familiar names like Zak Foster and Sheri Schumacher, I dove into the creative practices of many new artists to learn how improvisation had shaped and directed their craft. I wondered how connecting with such a wide-ranging group of creatives had inspired Jen.

EVER LOVING MEMORIES *(DETAIL)*
2020

SEEING RED / FEELING BLUE
2020

"It has been a gift and a wonderful way to connect with artists whose work I admire and has pushed me outside my comfort zone to do so. It has been a huge inspiration in learning that, yes, most artists work with improvisation (I just knew it!), and when you learn that there are so many ways to work with it, you begin to trust more and more that your way is just as good. It has helped me be confident in my own process and given me so many new ideas and different ways to try working. Plus, I love that I am able to share what I love and what I am learning. This is why I do most of the creative work that I do, to share and connect with others."

"My intention is to inspire others to look at the world around them more carefully, more mindfully, to see the extraordinary in the discarded, to notice the beauty in the mundane, and if they can't see it, to show them it is possible to look inward and to see things in a new and different way. It is possible to find and share the beauty you hold inside. How we see the world and what we share shapes our lives, our relationships, our actions."

Like myself, Jen is easily inspired. She finds inspiration everywhere and has a great affinity with makers of the past. She describes them, as well as her own past encounters, as "influencing everything that I see and do." Fashion, design, and architecture have all been important sources of inspiration, though, as Jen explains, what inspires our work may not always be obvious at the time.

"Often the things that inspire us are not immediately evident. I think the trick is to trust our interests in whatever it is that is captivating us. From a conversation with a friend, to a lyric in a song, to the pattern on the sidewalk . . . take it all in and the important stuff will resurface. Even the seemingly unimportant stuff has potential to have impact later. We are all right where we need to be, absorbing exactly what it is we need. The gift is to believe it, to learn from the hard stuff and act on what we have learned."

Through my conversations with Jen, I have learnt that she firmly believes in the idea of daily dedicated time to explore one's creativity. She has always been a proponent of play and learnt early on in life that the good stuff comes from trusting our instincts and following our curiosities. When I began my improvised journey, this is something I found highly productive. Whilst the majority of pieces that came from this play turned into nothing more, a small few proved to be the seedlings of something much bigger. Jen uses this idea of daily play to help overcome any creative slumps she may encounter.

"I'm a huge believer in daily playing, making something small for no reason at all, and it is a godsend to creative block. I'm just emerging from a creative funk. But, as I was going through the funk I never stopped making, playing creatively with something. During this time, I talked to a lot of people and received a lot of good advice, about not being too hard on myself and many suggestions to take a more complete break, so I think we all deal with it differently. What worked for me this time very likely might not work next time. And there will be a next time. The key is to not give up and be gentle with yourself as you go through it. It is a part of the creative cycle and it will pass."

Jen's renewed creative journey began thanks to the #the100dayproject: a global art project during which thousands of people commit to one hundred days of creating. During 2021, Jen shared her Continuations on Instagram. These small pieces, created from offcuts of bigger projects and experiments, reiterate the idea that even if some of our explorations don't flourish, the time spent is never wasted. The snippets of quilted fabric, joined together by visible zigzag stitching, create wonderful interactions and juxtapositions of colour and shape. During the time she was working on these pieces, I asked Jen to elaborate on the project.

"I have not always participated but usually do and have even created my own daily making projects when #the100dayproject is not going on. I had been playing around with collaging my saved quilt scraps and am happy that it dawned on me to do this every day for the project. I am loving how each one is turning out and they are a joy to put together. I love the idea of creating something from the scrap pile and continuing the life of the material, keeping it from landfill."

During the first countrywide lockdown in the UK, I worked daily on a project as a way to channel my energy and provide respite from the uncontrollable situation that was unfolding. This project would evolve into my temperature quilt. Through the many moments of reflection that making this piece afforded, I learnt a lot about myself, both as a quilter and as a member of society. I wonder if Jen too found that by dedicating a little of her practice to the same meditative steps, she discovered new things about herself.

"I'd say I learn more about myself and that turns into what I want to do with the work. The process is meditative and I enjoy it. It gives me time to process my thoughts and, oh my, there has been so much to process in the past few years! So, part of how I am making now is pretty straightforward but little decisions are being made along the way, just at a slower pace. It has been good with everything that has been going on outside of my little bubble and the daily project has been my way to keep the improvisational work fresh and playful."

RHYTHM IN BLUE *(DETAIL)*
2020

CHRIS ENGLISH

HUDDERSFIELD, ENGLAND

After an absence of a year, The Festival of Quilts, Europe's largest quilting and patchwork show, retuned to Birmingham's NEC in August 2021. As I walked amongst the competition quilts on display, I recognised a piece by Chris English. Titled On Me Head Giggsy, the focus of the piece was a duvet cover featuring the footballer Ryan Giggs, pieced alongside improv nine patches and Rupert the Bear fabric. The quilt was quintessentially Chris, who loves using found and recycled fabrics. He is an advocate of the sustainable sewing that is becoming more and more popular in quilt making as people attempt to reduce their impact on the planet. Like his Instagram handle, Chris' quilting output is similarly satisfying. As I continued to take in the competition entries, I saw many more of his quilts, each a visual feast. I'd seen these quilts in various stages of construction through social media, so to view them up close and personal was a real treat. Chris' list of inspiration is rich and varied. It may be for this reason that he produces so many quilts, which often feature an improvised take on traditional blocks such as four patches, nine patches, and half square triangles. He loves street art, especially when colours, pattern, and scale clash. The fashion designer Paul Smith, with his quirky take on British-ness, is also a big inspiration. Chris likens the ethos of punk music, with its energy and directness, to making a quilt.

"The DIY approach meant anyone could be part of the punk scene and if you wanted to form a band you could. I think it's the same for quilts."

FLIGHT *(DETAIL)*
2020

Perhaps most evident from his work is the inspiration Chris takes from vintage quilts and makers of the past. Like many improv quilters, he discovered the Gee's Bend quilts early on and has admired them ever since.

"I often use these quilts as inspiration and not always specifically from a visual perspective. Sometimes seeing them just encourages me to try something different. Rosie Lee Tompkins has also had a big influence on my work. I love the mix of fabric and imagery, and the size of the quilts. I find them truly beautiful."

In 2019 Chris attended QuiltCon in Nashville, Tennessee, where a number of pieces from the Marjorie Childress Collection were on display. This group of approximately 300 quilts has a strong emphasis on design and narrative, an emphasis clearly seen in Chris' own work. The use of different textiles throughout the collection, including clothing, wool, and denim, is another element that resonates. At The Festival of Quilts, I remember being inspired by the snippets of curtains, jeans, and bedcovers that Chris had used. Fabric which would have otherwise become landfill was repurposed and renewed with bold spontaneity. In one of his earlier quilts, vivid orange overalls, stained with oil from the previous owner's occupation, were pieced into improv triangles during an Instagram tour for my book, 'Inspiring Improv'. Chris explains his use of reclaimed textiles with an evident passion.

"I love saving fabric from landfill. I've used a mix of old clothes, but the most unusual fabric is from some of the old curtains that I find. The ones I really like are from the 60s and 70s and do not contain one natural fibre, but they do have amazing textures that contrast with the flat quilting cotton. Using these fabrics challenges me to use prints and patterns I might not normally buy, so I'm forced out of my comfort zone to try something different."

NEVER TRUST A TORY II
2022

I wanted to further understand Chris' reasons for choosing recycled textiles. In the past, such thriftiness was attributed to the lack of mass-produced fabrics. Nowadays, with so many new collections, I wondered what drew him to these types of fabric. Is it an ethical standpoint, or perhaps they have a more interesting story to tell? For Chris, there are many reasons.

"I'm not really into using patterns and prescribed fabrics, so this approach is perfect. Saving fabric from landfill is also important. Cotton is pretty intensive in its manufacture and there's plenty of fabric out there to use up. Whilst I occasionally buy new fabric, I don't feel the need to buy a new collection each season. Sometimes I find unfinished quilt tops which I love to add to my own. I think these quilts have an interesting story and by including them in my work, I hope to prolong the life of that fabric."

With his love of flea markets and charity shops providing a rich and eclectic array of fabric he may not otherwise encounter, it's not surprising that Chris' work is bold and vibrant. He describes part of his process as *"pushing the boat out and trying something different"*. The way he fearlessly combines prints, colours, and textures whilst still honouring the provenance of the fabric is truly inspiring. I love the additional layers of interest he adds to his pieces through big stitch hand quilting, tying, and embroidery. It's exciting to think of all the as-yet undiscovered fabric out there and what it could become in Chris' hands.

F**K OFF BORIS *(DETAIL)*
2022

TARA FAUGHNAN

OAKLAND, CALIFORNIA, USA

There are some quilters whose work stops me in my tracks. I mean, the kind of attention grabbing that makes you not want to move until you've taken in the whole quilt. Tara Faughnan is one such quilter. Some time ago, I think as far back as 2015, I fell down an Instagram rabbit hole and found myself in awe of a Double Wedding Ring quilt posted to Tara's feed. The quilt was in the collection of Roderick Kiracofe, quilt collector, curator, and author of 'Unconventional & Unexpected: American Quilts Below the Radar 1950 - 2000', and had recently been shown at an exhibition of Kiracofe's collection in Sonoma, California. Made by an unknown African American quilter, Tara credited this stunning quilt as ushering her onto a whole new creative path.

A few days later, a new post appeared on my Instagram feed that showed the beginnings of a Double Wedding Ring quilt. This was Tara's version, inspired by the unattributed quilt she had seen in the Kiracofe collection. The blocks were hand pieced and composed of a wondrously saturated palette. Right then, my love affair with her use of colour began.

Tara's quilting journey started in 2001. Using a reprint of the 1931 edition of '101 Patchwork Patterns' by Ruby Short McKim as a guide, she spent many happy weeks tracing around cardboard templates and cutting out pieces with a pair of scissors, unaware that rotary cutters, rulers, and plastic templates existed. With the familiarity of those paper templates, Tara's exploration of improvisation did not happen straight away.

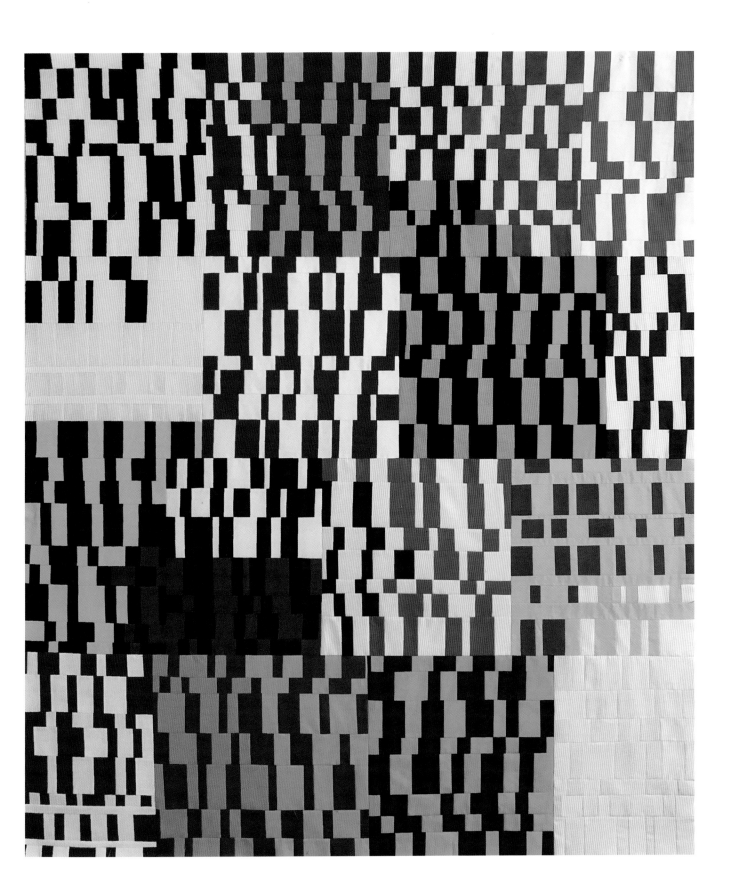

HITCH
2021

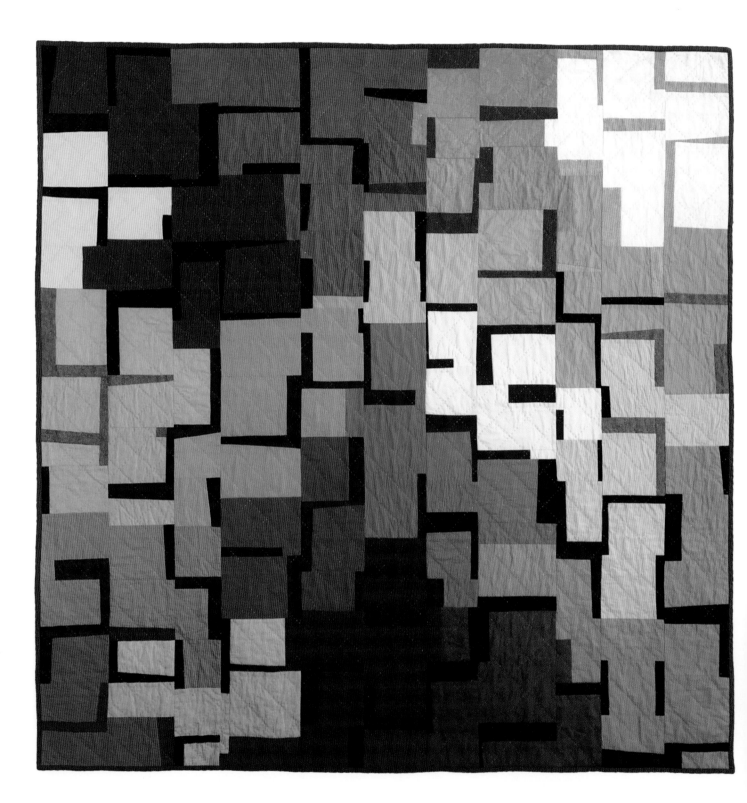

"I'm just now starting to become more comfortable with this style of working. I think my difficulty is with the definition of improv. There's improv in the colour process, there's improv in the composition process, and there's improv in the piecing process. I'm really comfortable with the first two, but like to have a general idea of where I'm going before I begin piecing."

Though she does not work in an improvised style exclusively, many of her traditional quilts have been inspired by a more liberated approach.

"I consider myself a traditional quilter at heart and I love vintage quilts. I find inspiration in forms, shapes, and the place where two seams meet. I draw a lot of inspiration from the simple bold geometry of antique quilts, and the wonderful disruption of pattern found in unconventional and improvisational quilts. My use of colour and contrasting values in all my work is directly inspired by these works."

In her quilts, Tara combines colours in the most eclectic way and believes this interaction to be the key inspiration that drives her and her creative practice. *"It's that intuitive moment when you put two colours together, and then two more, and two more, that I focus on."* Through such complex interactions she attempts to *"find the line that exists somewhere between harmony and discord and still make everything work together as a whole."* As creatives, especially when staring out, we often learn through how-to books, tutorials, or another's way of working that colours should be harmoniously combined. Many take this to mean that too many colours should not be thrown together and that there must always be a strict adherence to the colour wheel. I know from my own practice that combining colours one usually would not, can make the most exciting interactions. Tara's quilts are rich and full of vibrancy, though somewhat surprisingly, for her, the process doesn't start with colour.

GIVE AND TAKE
2020

"It's slightly different for every quilt, but usually I start with a shape or feeling I'd like to convey, rather than a palette. I find the shape of the block I'm working with has a large effect on the colours I will end up using. The reverse is also true. If I have a certain palette in mind, I will think of the shape that best plays to what I'm trying to express with those colours. I usually have an idea of what I want to create, but often quilts have a mind of their own, and the final outcome might not end up looking like what I was imagining in my head."

I know all too well the feeling of having a quilt divert from what you had originally envisaged. In the case of my How to Age a Tree quilt, my answer to such an obstacle was to cut the quilt in half, though I doubt many quilters would take such drastic action! For Tara, distancing herself from a piece that may not be turning out the way she imagined is one way of dealing with a creative roadblock.

"If I'm stuck, I've learned to keep going and keep creating. I probably won't be making favourite quilts when I feel stuck, but I try to divorce myself from the product and just focus on the process. It's really quite freeing when you can separate from caring about the outcome. I figure I can take the lessons forward rather than trying to finesse the present piece."

LAZY GAL
2016

ZAK FOSTER

BROOKLYN, NEW YORK, USA

Zak Foster was always the creative child. Like myself, he experimented with many different media throughout his childhood and teenage years, flitting from paint to pottery, drawing to engraving, before settling on textiles after his first quilt led to another. He describes fabric as *"a very distinct media"* owing to its familiarity and relatability. I first became aware of Zak in 2014. Raised in rural North Carolina, his work draws on Southern textile traditions, with an approach to design than is both intuitive and improvisational. I was attracted to his bold compositions, which often feature a limited colour palette. The size of his pieces was impressive too, often including himself in progress shots as an indicator of scale. Here was a quilter whose work I wanted to see more of.

Zak's quilts are made with a zero-waste approach. His use of reclaimed textiles affords a liberating lack of control and often extends to repurposing the thread found in the seams of old clothing. He sources materials from thrift stores and readily accepts donations from friends if they are decluttering. It is from his eclectic stash that the ideas for his quilts first stem, preferring to use fabrics and colours as initial sources of inspiration.

"I usually start with a few colours. I sort through fabric and choose pieces I'm drawn to, then add more to round out the selection. The process then involves unsewn pieces being arranged in different ways. I play until something catches my eye. Then, I try to capture it, to twist and change it. I let the fabrics inform the process as much as possible."

SEA GLASS *(DETAIL)*
2021

TREY 1
65" X 85"
2020

His colourful statement pieces are certainly eye-catching; evocative of the quilts of Gee's Bend, which, unsurprisingly, Zak too takes inspiration from. He enjoys the work of Irene Williams for the *"whimsical and unapologetic repurposing"* evident in her quilt Strips, made from deconstructed basketball jerseys. The irregular shapes of Loretta Pettway Bennet's quilts are another favourite.

Alongside the quilts made from his own fabric, Zak specialises in memory quilts, undertaking commissions from those looking to solidify memories of friends and relatives into an heirloom quilt. Most of these commissions are made to honour a recently deceased loved one, though Zak has also made them as a retirement gift and for someone adopting their first child. He describes these quilts as *"many layered monuments"* and enjoys the getting to know the person through repurposing the clothes they wore, which he believes are infused with their energy. Such collaborations rely on trust and are acts of preservation. The use of such fabrics ensures a different creative path each time, allowing for a spontaneous and organic practice.

More recently, Zak has begun to make burial quilts, a natural extension and progression of the memory quilt. The idea is that during your life you charge the fabric with memories, before it is then used to cover your body when you die, providing comfort and solace. Shrouding the dead is an age-old tradition and something that society has shied away from in favour of a more clinical, sterile practice. The subject is certainly taboo, yet as Zak mentioned in a recent interview, we comfort babies not by putting them in a metal or wooden box, but by swaddling them with blankets. Why shouldn't the same be done to comfort our loved ones when they pass? Or even ourselves? Zak has a quilt that he plans to use for his burial and has become an *"active participant"* in what is inevitable for us all.

Like many other improvisers, Zak also uses quilting to rally and call to action. During the first one hundred days of the Trump administration, he worked on pieces that highlighted the unrest and the resistance many people felt during that time. Phrases such as *"grab the arc of justice and bend"* and *"a great America requires all of us"* were appliquéd onto blocks and pieced together into a quilt Zak describes as *"a first love letter to my country"* and is a stirring acknowledgment that there is much work to be done in order to create a fair and just society. The quilt is emotional and thought-provoking.

I have Zak to thank for one of the most significant and emotional pieces of patchwork I have made during my time as a quilter. On the 7th March 2016, which happened to be my birthday, Zak put a call out for quilters to participate in the construction of a social activism quilt. After a trip to Mexico, he'd learnt of forty-three male students from the Ayotzinapa Rural Teachers' College who, on 26th September 2014, were taken into custody by police officers and never seen again. As I learnt more about the disappearance of these young men, I knew I had to contribute to this project. I myself had turned to quilting as a balm during difficult moments in my own life. If I could in some small way offer comfort to the parents of those who disappeared and help to highlight their plea, I knew it was so important to put my hands to work.

César Manuel González Hernández was nineteen years old and a second-year student at Ayotzinapa when he disappeared. I made my block using red and white fabric to spell his name in improv letters. Like the other contributors to the 43 for 43 quilt, I didn't know this man, yet felt connected to him by the slow and mediative piecing. I found out as much as I could about César. I learnt that, like me, he was fond of animals. He was energetic and passionate about kickboxing and riding bulls at the rodeo. My block honouring César was combined with the forty-two others, to create a protest banner, each naming a student, as well as six blocks honouring the bystanders whose lives were lost on the same night.

Zak delivered the banner to the parents of the missing students in September 2016, weeks before the second anniversary of the disappearance of their sons. On the 26th of each month they march in a continual fight for justice and to break the silence that has surrounded the case. Despite their actions, little has changed. Ongoing work continues in Mexico for the betterment of Mexicans through such organisations as Ayuda en Acción, a nonprofit group working to improve access to education for children, as well as for the rights of women and workers in rural communities.

43 FOR 43
2016

MARCO
ANTONIO
GÓMEZ
MOLINA

43 FOR 43

ABEL GARCÍA HERNÁNDEZ

ORIGEN: TECUNAPA
SITUACIÓN: DESAPARECIDO

Luis
Ángel
Francisco
Arzola

CHRIS
TON
COL
GAR

¿DONDEESTAS? ¿DONDEESTAS? ¿DONDEESTAS? ¿DONDEESTAS?

Jorg
Aníb
Cru
Mend

JOSÉ ÁNGEL
AMPOS CANTOR

ésaR GONZÁLEZ
ANUEL HERNÁNDEZ

orlos Hernández
M.

el frijolito

Luis
Ángel
Francisco
Arzola

ALVAREZ
NAVA

RODR
TLA

CHRISTIAN
TOMÁS
COLÓN
GARNICA

¿DONDE ESTAS? ¿DONDE ESTAS? ¿DONDE ESTAS? ¿DONDE ESTAS? ¿DONDE ESTAS?

MARTIN
Getsemany
Sánchez
Garcia

Jorge
Aníbal
Cruz
Mendoza

BERNARDO
FLORES
ALCARAZ

Julia

Lg

TRUJILLO

JONÁS
GONZÁLEZ

ángel
Abanca
Carrillo

NY
EZ
PA

El
ero
éz

felipe
Arnulfo
Rosa

José
Luis
Luna
Torres

Jorge
Antonio
Tizapa
Poideón

ABELARDO

VÁZQUEZ

PENITEN

Ghostnani Izquierdo de la Cruz

El Magda

BENJAMIN
ASCENCIO
BAUTISTA

NAV

JOSE
EDUARDO
BARTOLO
TLATEMPA

MARCIAL
PABLO
BARANDA

LEONEL
CASTRO
ABARCA

MIGUEL
ÁNGEL
MENDOZA
ZACARÍAS

JOSE ÁNGEL
AVARRETE GONZÁLEZ

43

PEPE

Christian Alfonso

Rodriguez Telumbre

DORIAM
GONZÁLEZ
PARRAL

JORGE
LUIS
GONZÁLEZ
PARRAL

Carlos
Ramirez

DEDICADO A LOS 43 Y A LOS OT
MILES Y A QUIENES LOS AMA

Adán
Abrajan

ANTONIO
SANTANA

Migu

Áng

Herná

Mauricio
Ortega
Valerio

Emiliano
Alen Gaspar
de la CRUZ

Giovanni
Galindo
Guerrero
43

Saúl
Bruno
Sørõ

Israel
Jacinto
Lugardo

CUTBERT
ORTIZ
RAMOS

eal

LUKE HAYNES

LOS ANGELES, CALIFORNIA, USA

"I make fine art with a process that historically has only been identified with grandmas and crafts," says Luke Haynes of his work. In this summing-up, the architect-turned-quilter touches on two points that have long been debated within the quilting community. When I began quilting, I naively believed that I must be the only man doing it. The world in which I found myself was so female orientated. The quilting books I read were written by women, as were the patterns and magazine articles. The fabric collections that were finding their way into my stash were designed by women. I remember visiting one quilt shop early on and noticing a chair positioned in the corner, upon which a sign was propped that read, 'Husbands Wait Here'. I couldn't help but wonder if a man visited the shop with his wife, with the purpose of satisfying his own need for fabric, how he might feel reading that.

With a view to meeting more like-mined people, I created an Instagram account in 2012. It served first and foremost as a way of documenting my process and the quilts I was making, but through social media I soon began to make connections with other quilters, some of whom were men. Initially I was surprised, though looking back now, I'm not sure why. As my social circle grew, I continued to discover male quilters, each contributing to this female-dominated world through their own quilt making. Most were traditional, whilst a few were working in more liberated ways. One such quilter was Luke.

AMERICAN CONTEXT #73 - NICOLE'S WORLD
2018

JOY 3
2020

Luke was my first quilt crush. His work resonated with me on so many levels. His quilts were so different to all the others I had seen up to that point and they opened my eyes to a whole new way of defining what it meant to quilt and be a quilter. He rightly describes his work as fine art, which was something I never imagined a quilt could be. It was his portrait quilts that first commanded my attention. Full of impact, they combine traditional quilt blocks with appliqué portraits, often made from the clothes of the sitter. These collisions of traditional and modern have been showcased in art galleries and exhibitions worldwide. Evidently, the work stands for itself and is well-deserving of accolade, yet I wondered if Luke believed gender played a role in his success and how he is viewed as a quilter.

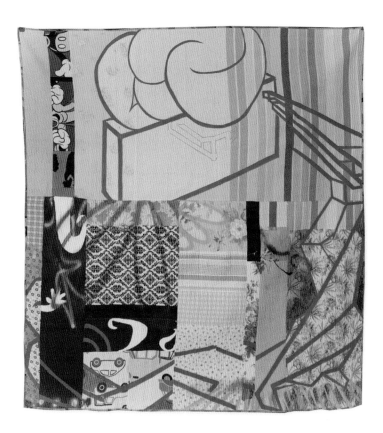

QUILTLLABORATION #7 - CLOUDS
2016

"I will always be an outsider. When I was first starting, I wasn't invited and when I got successes I was often looked at as a pariah, assuming that my successes were due to gender and not my work. I will say to the credit of those observers, there is a shred of truth there. I have had shows that were gender-based but I would like to think that the vast majority of my work and value is in my making and not as much my novelty. This is less and less as time goes on. There are far more male quilters and I don't hear as much about that anymore."

Luke studied architecture at Cooper Union in New York City. *"I was interested in exploring structure and material; the things that I valued the most when experienced spatially. I wanted to create environments that offered what my upbringing hadn't; ones that were crafted to care for the inhabitant and regenerate themselves. I grew my knowledge of what it meant to create one's own system of comfort through tangible structures during my time there, but ended up leaving, still searching for a better way to fulfil my 'why'."*

That fulfilment would come in the form of quilting. Luke taught himself to sew and found solace in creating what he describes as the *"epitome of a comfort object."*

"I found intrigue and success in challenging how people perceived the traditional paradigm of craft. I treated quilts as sculpture, created photo-realistic portraits out of fabric, and constructed large scale quilts to cover external building structures."

Luke acknowledges the overlaps that exist in architecture and quilting and credits the architectural foundation established at Cooper Union in guiding how he manipulates textiles. Both disciplines have a deep appreciation of the form of function, with his architecture background giving Luke the "confidence to grant myself permissions to experiment in ways that have been historically taboo in the world of quilting."

QUILTLLABORATION #8
HAYNES AND PARKS
2016

CLOTHES QUILT #7
CAMERA
2016

QUILTLLABORATION #11 - FLYING GEESE
2018

These experiments have shaped an impressive body of work, subverting the traditional through texture, shape, and colour. Despite his evident comfortableness with the technique, Luke did not start off creating in an improvised way. As a self-confessed analytical thinker, it was through his collaborations with Joe Cunningham that he learnt to be free and allow the fabric to be part of the conversation. This conversation often addresses sustainability, with reclaimed and recycled fabrics featuring heavily in his quilts. His use of clothing and household fabrics adds the stories of those who once used the fabrics to his own and that of the quilt. In 2016, having both been invited to teach at an improv quilting retreat in Michigan, we spent time before the classes, scouring the racks of the local Goodwill for shirts in every style and colour. A few hours later, these were deconstructed, sliced into, and sewn together in a riotous display of improvised making. The students greatly enjoyed the process and it was eye-opening for me to see fabric used in this way.

In a more recent collaboration with wife Nicole, Luke's series of Joy Quilts once again showcases an eclectic fabric mix and are some of my favourites that he has produced. Made during a time when the world needed a little more happiness, these pieces are vibrant and fun. Luke's pieced fabrics provide a canvas for Nicole's embellishments: bold, organic shapes cut from various textiles and appliquéd to the quilt.

When beginning a new quilt, Luke starts with what he wants to say with the piece. What is very clear to me is that Luke is both an artist who makes quilts and a quilter who makes art. With pieces in the International Quilt Museum and the Norton Collection, as well as private collections, Luke's quilts show that these utilitarian objects are equally deserving of a place on the artistic stage, to be held to the same standard as other media. Despite his success, he still encounters hurdles getting people to accept and show his work.

"I find that it is my job, far more than making quilts, to educate people on why quilts can be valuable and interesting beyond novelty. There are a lot of people doing that now and that helps. Quilts have inborn nostalgic and functional value, but the monetary value is often overlooked."

DEBBIE JESKE

SEATTLE, WASHINGTON, USA

I find quilters to be a sharing sort. This has never been more evident than in today's internet-fuelled world. Our social media platforms abound with community spirit, as quilters trade work and words through bees, blog hops, and virtual retreats. Despite where you live, connections can be made across continents and new friendships forged with a few simple clicks. It was through this sense of community that I first discovered Debbie Jeske, though I have to admit it was her Instagram handle, not her quilts, that first caught my attention.

Too many years have passed for me to recall the exact details, yet I remember an immediate sense of comfort when I first scrolled upon the words 'A Quilter's Table'. My mind was immediately transported back to a time when quilting communities would gather in person, around a table or quilt frame, and work collaboratively on a quilt. The name was nostalgic and inviting. I was eager to learn more about Debbie and her quilts.

It's no surprise that Debbie relishes being active in the online quilting community. She enjoys creating a variety of sewn projects, though it is in improvisational quilt-making that she finds a special joy. It was through the online community that she first became aware of the technique.

LOOSELY CONNECTED *(DETAIL)*
2018

*"I was a very traditional quilter for over twenty years and discovered
the modern quilting movement in 2010. Exposure to the internet and
the discovery of quilt blogs made my quilting world so much bigger.
In discovering modern quilting, I saw things I never knew existed.
I began to explore improvisational quilt-making by taking classes
and joining groups with a similar interest."*

One such group is Bee Sewcial, an improv-only quilting bee. Each
month, participants work on a theme set by one member, creating
blocks or units that sit within a set of expected parameters. These
may include colour, shape, or size, though such expectations do not
limit the creativity of the contributors, who improvise in varying
styles. Once the completed contributions are sewn together, the
resulting quilts are maximalist and bold, with loud-yet-curated
interactions of pattern and colour, and the once separate units
exude a sense of pleasing cohesiveness. The work that comes
from such a bee is inspiring, not only in prompting others to
explore improvisation, but also to form new groups where ideas
of teamwork and experimentation can flourish, as Debbie explains.

REDWORK *(DETAIL)*
2021

REWORK
2019

"I am strongly motivated by the quilting community, as well as being hugely inspired by it. Whether it's a small group like a bee, or the larger community, I find such inspiration and motivation in seeing and sharing our work with each other. With Bee Sewcial in particular, I've discovered new ways of thinking about inspiration, and much more frequently explore improv with intent."

With her collaborative work often inspired by an initial prompt, I was curious to find out what other sources inform Debbie's quilt-making and how much of that inspiration comes from past makers. Like myself, she has found focus in places one would not expect, once using bacon as a prompt for her bee mates. Like my own cabbage quilts, this unusual starting point solidifies the idea that through improv quilting, an object, an idea, or a feeling can be expressed in fabric, either literally or through suggestions of line, shape, and colour.

"I may find inspiration in a colour palette, a traditional quilt block or design, a technique, or even a specific item found in my surroundings. I feel a good portion of my work is inspired by makers of the past in some way, though the end point may be quite different from what I was initially inspired by, with the original inspiration difficult to see."

After the release of 'Inspiring Improv', many versions of the book's projects began to appear on Instagram. I was particularly impressed by Debbie's interpretation of a Tuscan Pom, which used techniques from my Warholian Cabbage quilt.

The quilt, which for Debbie evokes fond memories of seeing her first pomegranate tree, is everything I love about improv piecing: quirky, unique, and an outlet for escapism.

Looking at her creative output, Debbie's quilts have these qualities in abundance. Collectively, there is a consistent look and feel to the work, though she describes her process as feeling unique with each quilt, often beginning with intent, yet, at other times, embracing the spontaneity of fabric play. Her design wall becomes home for the units she pieces within her current parameters, allowing compositions to change and shift organically. I have often waxed lyrically about the importance of my design wall, not only in practical terms, but also as a way of providing that all-important distance between yourself and the quilt in progress, when things are a little mired. Debbie embraces this idea of time and patience.

"Sometimes it's just a matter of patiently waiting, for either the right time or the right idea to strike. Leaving a work in progress up on my design wall where I can see it each day eventually leads me to the needed solution, or at least a way to move forward. Starting a new project can often be just what's needed to un-stick things, especially if it's a project with very few limits. Piecing from scraps is another way to keep creating when the 'real' project needs some time to 'marinate'."

YAY OR NAY
2019

HEIDI PARKES

MILWAUKEE, WISCONSIN, USA

Heidi Parkes lives a handmade lifestyle, sewing her own clothes, fermenting, eating from pottery she made a decade ago, and practicing hand yoga (yes, it's a thing, and I can attest to its benefit). Atop her website, her name is followed by the words 'Artist, Quilts, and Mending'. This order is fitting, for although it was her quilts which first attracted my attention, I soon discovered the beautiful handwork she applies to clothes and other worn objects to revive them and prolong their life. I saw how she uses darning and reweaving to mend threadbare and moth-damaged jeans. Heidi describes the mending process as *"giving love"* back to a garment that has given so much to the wearer. As I explored more and more of Heidi's skillfully repaired pieces, I became enamoured with her use of stitch and the warm nostalgia it awoke in me. Growing up, visits to my grandmother's house would invariably result in my asking to see her darning mushroom. I was fascinated with this small, wooden object, yet at the time couldn't quite understand its use. Seeing Heidi's darning for the first time transported me back to watching my grandmother's hands work yarn in a similar way. As well as quilter and repairer, to me, Heidi is first and foremost an artist.

A BREATH HAS FOUR PARTS *(DETAIL)*
2020

MEUSE, PANDEMIC, INVISIBLE, SWEETHEART
2020

For her, quilting has a family connection. Before Heidi's arrival in 1982, her grandmother organised a collaborative family quilt to commemorate her birth. This set the tone for a life centred on the handmade. She was raised in a home where sewing, mending, cooking, canning, woodworking, photography, ceramics, painting, and plasterwork were the norm. How wonderful to be exposed to so many expressions of creativity, which clearly influenced a young Heidi. The quilts she makes tug at memories and shared experience and she names her grandmother as one of her many inspirations.

"I'm sure that a great deal of my inspiration comes from past and contemporary makers in a variety of mediums. My grandmother, parents, teachers, professors, mentors, friends, and sweethearts have all played a role. Many contemporary makers, authors, and those long since departed whom I've never met have inspired me too. The paintings of Philip Guston and Julie Mehretu were front of mind for me in 2016, when I became obsessed by the way they scraped or wiped away paint. I wanted to create a "ghost" like that in my quilts too, and that allowed me to innovate the 4-layered transparent surfaced quilts that I made, like But, I Tried to Remember. *That particular quilt was also inspired by my ex-fiancé, Marcel Proust's Remembrance of Things Past, Sex and the City, the Piecework Collective* Colour *exhibition, my broken sewing machine, the Korean Patchwork techniques I learned in Seoul because of my favourite college roommate Youngok Kim, and the exposed knots on a Rachel Carey George quilt that lives at the Milwaukee Art Museum."*

With such an eclectic source of inspiration, it's no surprise that Heidi's quilts are rich and full of detail. For me, many of her pieces are wonderfully calming, thanks in part to their ethereal quality. To achieve the ghost, Heidi layers fabrics, threads, yarns, and ribbons beneath larger pieces of silk organza scrim, which she then secures into position using hand quilting. To feel like I'm viewing these quilts through a fine mist, my connection to them is greater than it would be if all the individual elements were clearly defined. My eyes work harder, pause more, and appreciate the small nuances that are hidden in the handwork. But, I Tried to Remember was awarded third place for handwork at QuiltCon 2018. In a more recent finish, Heidi incorporated into a corner of her quilt what many would discard: thread trimmings, packaging twine, yellow strands from opening up a vintage feed sack. These form "*a collection of colours and textures*" that she herself could never compose on her own.

Heidi masterfully uses textiles, such as tablecloths, bed linens, gifted fabric, and travel finds, to add subtle meaning and material memory to her quilts. With the raw materials being so varied, I wondered if the process she adopts when beginning a quilt changes with each new piece.

"I think that at its core, the process I follow is quite familiar. I begin by watching for things that interest me and I look for serendipitous connections: a point of curiosity, an upcoming exhibition opportunity, a technique I'd like to try, a series I want to expand on, an event in my personal life, an availability of interesting materials, etc. When I feel I've combined enough ideas together, and time is on my side, I'll green-light a particular project that's been living in the back of my mind. It's usually my preference then to yield to my circumstances of time, materials, workspace, and the like to stay on track with my plan. If I can, I'll work on that project to the exclusion of all else, preferring to spend a week at the computer, followed by a week of sewing so that I can keep my focus without distractions. However, if I have to sew whenever I can catch a minute, or in between projects, that'll become part of the art. I'll hand piece, baste, hand quilt, bind, embroider my name on the back, take photographs, and sew on a sleeve."

Heidi clearly loves to work in an improvised way. She admits she was *"the most engaged and curious"* when working in the style in the early 2010s, regardless of what medium she was creating in. An introduction to the Japanese aesthetic of wabi-sabi by a professor of ceramics during her freshman year at The School of the Art Institute floated the idea of *"a collaboration with nature, an appreciation for the ephemeral, and the possibility of the perfect mistake."*

"I was encouraged to notice my scrap pile as much as my assignment. Extraordinary insights could be found in the way I organised my tools and wedged clay. Of course, clay was a favourite medium of mine before art school too. My maternal grandmother lived in Santa Fe, New Mexico where she owned a kiln and a garage ceramics studio. She taught me that sometimes the 'Kiln Gods' had a mind of their own. We had to cultivate an image of what we wanted to make, alongside an openness to possibility, when I visited her for a week or two at a time in elementary school. These twin mindsets allowed us to dream and avoid disappointment simultaneously."

"Inherently in quilting, I am so often struck by the transformation that takes place between piecing and quilting. I see before and after photos of quilt tops and quilts, and I think that the Kiln Gods live here too. It makes me think that as much as any quilter might think of themselves as a planner, that we all have an improv side, that we must anticipate the magic that happens when three layers unite."

I adore the idea that the final outcome of a quilt is not entirely in our hands. I often talk about how fabric has a mind of its own and how it wants to shift and transform as you try your best to control it. Being open to this, to change, and to the will of the 'Quilt Gods', is rewarded by unexpected yet welcomed creativity.

BUT, WHAT WAS IT LIKE? *(DETAIL)*
2018

A FASHION FROM Irvine's

DREW STEINBRECHER

CINCINNATI, OHIO, USA

My first exposure to the work of Drew Steinbrecher came in 2015 when I saw his piece Urban/Suburban. This wonderfully expressive quilt was inspired in part by Over-the-Rhine, the Cincinnati neighbourhood where Drew works, famed for its historic buildings and ornate brick façades. Coupled with his background in graphic design, architecture often works its way into Drew's multidisciplinary creative practice, which is bold and energetic.

As a self-confessed introvert, he nonetheless feels at home in the hustle and bustle of a city. In his quilts, I see the hurried pace of urban living, the to-ing and fro-ing of people, crossing and intersecting as they go about their work and play. Dwellings once again find their way into Tidy Towns, Irish Houses, a piece created after a holiday in Ireland. The brightly coloured houses are realised through rows and rows of colour blocks, each with windows and doors that add snippets of contrasting interest.

"I have always found inspiration in the chaos and energy of urban environments: graffiti, old walls with torn posters and flaking paint, dirty and grimy surfaces, power lines and poles, signage, crumbling concrete."

LINE STUDY NO. 9 - LIQUORICE ALLSORTS
2017

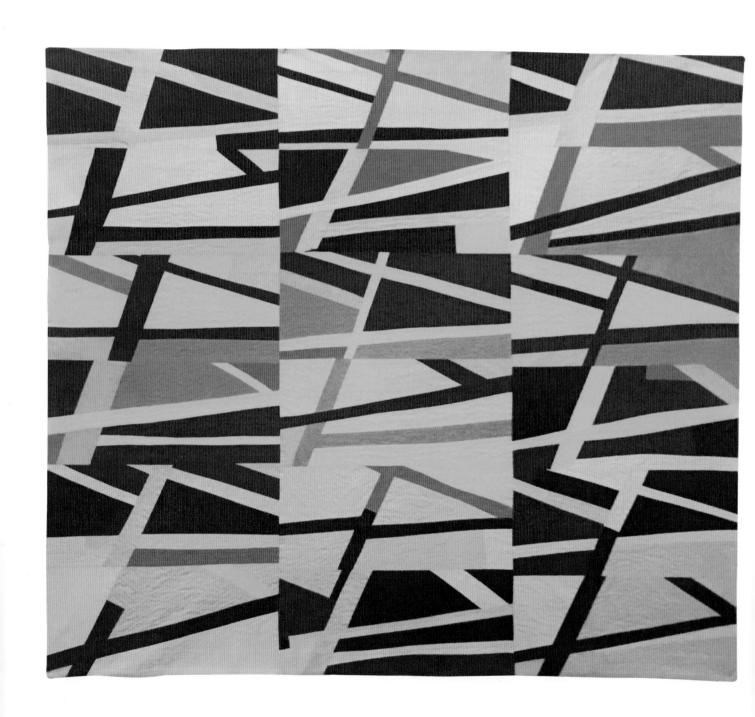

ONE-OFF THREE
2018

Drew adeptly transfers this energy into expressive piecing. His quilts are arresting with their movement and dynamic compositions. They share an underlying structure with the architecture he finds so inspiring. I'm always thrilled whenever new works by him appear in my Instagram feed. They command attention, with much for the eye to explore. My favourite quilts are those in which he creates crossroads of line and colour, focusing on varied repetition. These pieces, not surprisingly titled Crossroads, highlight Drew's mastery of the improvised technique. Despite having worked with his hands and being creative from a young age, it was only a relatively short time ago that Drew discovered quilting.

"I had always wanted to have total control over my work from the inception. In design school, a professor once told me I needed to let go and not be so rigid. Long story short, I discovered improv quilts online about ten years ago. That finally led me to try working improvisationally."

I was surprised to learn that as part of Drew's process, he takes to the computer to plan out a piece beforehand. He then moves to the design wall to pin fabric sections into place before sewing them together.

"I used to work one hundred percent improvisationally on my large quilt pieces. But recently I have found myself going back to the computer and working through a piece before I put anything on the design wall. It might change once I have something on the wall, but I do the initial work in Adobe Illustrator. This approach also allows me to work through the piecing and construction of a complex quilt."

Recently, the quilts on Drew's Instagram feed have shared the spotlight with his collages and prints. With the same improvisational approach, he uses printmaking not only to create exciting pieces, but to help become creatively unstuck.

"Changing mediums and working in my sketchbook helps me to move past creative blocks. I recently started collaging with mono-printed paper that I print on a gelatine press. It's different yet similar to working with fabric and quilting. Also, leaving the studio entirely... taking a walk, listening to music or watching TV, and taking a break from creative work, helps."

ONE-OFF ONE
2017

MELANIE TUAZON

LIVINGSTON, NEW JERSEY, USA

The bio at the top of Melanie Tuazon's Instagram profile reads *"I cut up fabric and sew it back together using thread and my feelings."* This is a sentiment that many improv quilters will be familiar with. An improv quilt can have much intent behind it, not only in the way it is made, but also in the message it conveys and the story it tells. Much of Melanie's work explores how modern domesticity, feminism, and identity intersect within the context of the quilting tradition. She expresses her aforementioned feelings through both planned and unplanned elements and uses a spectrum of improvisation which includes curves, skinny piecing, and occasional handwork. Melanie describes her way of improvising as an *"expression of self"* and believes everything she has done has informed her practice.

"Early on, I felt intimidated by the huge number of choices available to improvisers and designed many quilts in advance. After taking improvisation classes I found that many quilters whose work I loved improvise within parameters. I started figuring out how to improvise in ways I really enjoyed. When I found that I could customise my process and also make something unique I realised the artistry in expressing myself. I find that the improv process is a unique product of the choices we make in a given situation, that are rooted in our lived experience."

NEIGHBORS *(DETAIL)*
2017

When the time comes for such self-expression, Melanie's process is similar to my own. There are some who believe that an improv quilt is exclusively made in the moment, yet there can absolutely be forethought. Many of my quilts evolve from an initial inspiration source. For Melanie, that inspiration stems from familiar places.

"When I improvise, I am very introspective. I like to take uncomfortable thoughts and turn them into comfort objects. Many of my quilts are inspired by something in my life that is a little unsettling, and over the course of making them I process and come to terms with how I feel about it. I am very much inspired by makers of the past. I think of women whose only voice outside of their domestic world was their stitches. I think about the makers who developed the techniques and trends that are passed from generation to generation. The quilters of Gee's Bend inspired an entire generation of modern quilters with their improvisation, colours, and materials, including myself. I think about modern quilt artists like Chawne Kimber and Heidi Parkes who have been so generous as teachers and role models."

Each of Melanie's quilts starts with an idea, a technique, and a stack of fabric, though the order of how she decides on them is different for every quilt.

"Sometimes I have an idea and find the fabric to fit, other times I have a stack of fabric in colours that I want to play with."

Scrolling through her Instagram feed, how Melanie harnesses this inspiration into thought-provoking pieces is clear to see. I have always been enamoured by her bold piecing, particularly the freehand curves which I myself love to experiment with. We share a love of dense matchstick quilting, which she uses to contrast with the curving vortexes she pieces. Where these seams converge, each newly discovered moment trumps the last. One of my favourite works, her 2019 piece Unruly, represents the beauty found in resisting efforts to control our bodies and minds. Each time I view this piece I find something new. I wanted to know if Melanie finds it difficult to resist efforts to control the process when making a piece like this, or whether there is a trust from the beginning.

BLUE HOUSES
2018

"My trust in the process is something that I have to practice. There are times when I try to control the outcome too much, and the results will show me that it's time to let go. There is also a mental zone where I am completely tuned into my choices and actions, where I truly don't know what will happen, and there is delight in discovery. Where I fall on that spectrum will shows from time to time depending on my mental space and frequency of practice. But that's how improv helps me tune into my mindset and show me something I might not have noticed before."

Looking at Melanie's more recent work, I find myself becoming more and more inspired by her use of handwork. For a long time (until making some of the quilts for this book) I used a sewing machine exclusively to piece and quilt my quilts. Thanks to quilters like Melanie and Heidi Parkes, whose use of handwork is so captivating, my understanding of hand piecing and hand quilting has been redefined. For me, hand stitching is comforting to look at. It reminds me of my grandmother and the idea of make-do-and-mend. In 2021 Melanie's piece Taking Up Space (Do the Work) won second place in the handwork category at QuiltCon. The quilt represented four years of personal and reflective stitching, with the inner work visible on the outside. The jogakbo piecing, exposed knots, and distorted stitches serve as signs of the maker's imperfect hand. I asked Melanie if she saw these marks as a record of her, the maker, rather than the quilt, and wondered if they change or shift as she becomes more confident in a piece?

"I do see them as records of my hands. I hope that it makes viewers think about the person who made the piece, not just the fabric and thread. I improvise and sew by hand for that reason, to put individuality into a quilt. I see knots as a symbol of strength and vulnerability. They are usually hidden away, but they hold everything together."

When I've dedicated a large amount of time to a piece, I feel a mixture of emotions as completion draws near. For many of my quilts, particularly my most recent works which have been hand quilted or embellished in some way, I often struggle with deciding which stitch is the last. There is a duality between wanting the piece done, but not wanting to let go of something that has been a constant for however many weeks or months it has taken to get to that point. After spending so much time, how do we know when done is done? Melanie wonderfully describes this feeling as *"the click"*.

"I'm usually done with the quilt before it's done with me. I often get an idea for my next quilt before the current one is done and then the finish feels longer than it actually is. I am very interested in what I call 'the click'; the feeling that something is done and feels right. I am always listening for it, and when I hear it, I try not to second guess myself."

UNRULY
2019

Part Three: **NEXT**

Like anything that spans a great length of time, the history of improvised quilting is not one that can be easily recorded in its entirety. Whilst we have looked at a wide range of past and present makers, there will always be some who go unnoticed, amazing works that remain undiscovered. As I continue to research and expand my knowledge of quilting, I rejoice whenever I happen upon a maker who, hitherto, was unknown to me. A new name, a new style, a new choice of material; the vast and inspiring body of improv quilting is a treasure trove of discovery, collectively telling a most expressive story.

Looking forward, this story will continue to be told by those who have yet to attempt the style. Perhaps you are one of those people. The improv quilts you make will be added to the cannon and become part of the ever-growing history. My hope is that this final section of the book will provide a starting point and encourage you to create a quilt with purpose, one that moves beyond utility and can be considered both use and ornament.

As you may have deduced, you won't find comprehensive patterns or specific instructions for full quilts in this section, only tips and techniques to help you on your way. The aim is not to create a carbon copy of my quilts, but rather be inspired to tell a personal story in your own. To this end, for the projects that feature piecing techniques, such as Confetti and Streamers, specific quantities of fabric are not given. I have instead provided the dimensions of my finished quilt and listed the approximate quantities of fabric used.

You should therefore use this section as a starting point, rather than a directive. Think about what you want your quilt to say, to celebrate, highlight, or elevate. Adopt an attitude that permits you to be open about a change of direction, so that when you begin a project, you're not burdened down by the weight of expectation and are free to make spontaneous decisions. Use these techniques to make quilts as unique as your handwriting.

Alongside the quilt projects, you'll also find an overview of the tools and notions I used, as well as a section detailing the important relationship I have with my long arm quilter, Trudi Wood, whose stitches add to the story of my quilts as much as mine do.

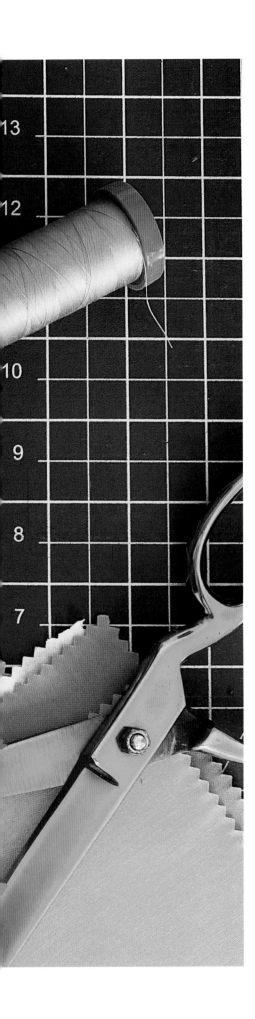

TOOLS AND NOTIONS

It is assumed that your interest in patchwork and quilting has already encouraged you to curate a basic toolkit, comprising of a sewing machine or hand sewing needle, thread, a rotary cutter, a self-healing cutting mat, a pair of fabric scissors, and an iron.

Throughout the course of making the quilts that follow, I pushed myself creatively and tried new and exciting techniques, sometimes necessitating the need for more specialised tools. I say specialised, yet what I really mean is things which I'd yet to use in my quilt making. For some of you, especially if your creative efforts span several disciplines, you may already have these things. What follows is a list of those tools and notions I found either a necessity or really useful. Before embarking on any of the techniques, read through the instructions fully to see if there is a specific piece of kit you may be missing.

FABRIC

Some of the techniques that follow move on from piecing and provide you with ways to embellish and finish your quilts. Where piecing is featured, this focuses on the process to make the units, rather than a whole quilt. Remember that for this reason, and because you will most likely want to explore your own ideas, specific quantities and measurements of fabric are not provided, save for the facing technique, where the amount of fabric needed is calculated using the perimeter of your quilt.

Many of the techniques, such as stuffed appliqués and the improv alphabet, lend themselves to smaller cuts or scraps, so unless you have a very specific colour scheme or fabric pull in mind, feel free to raid your stash. You may want to trial the technique first before committing to a full-sized project. Where I have used alternatives to cotton, these are mentioned in the story of the quilt. I encourage you to experiment with different fibres, as well as reclaimed and recycled textiles. Wool, linen, and denim can bring a wonderful tactile quality to your quilts, whilst more unusual fabrics, such as corduroy, velvet, organza, and other silks, can create real statement pieces. Old table linens, inherited or otherwise, home furnishings, and clothing all add history and significance to a quilt's story. Remember that the success of the fabric being sewn somewhat depends on the needle that it is sewn with. Be sure to choose an appropriate needle size and type for the fabric you are sewing.

THREAD

As well as a good quality thread for piecing, you may wish to have other thread weights to hand to experiment with quilting and embellishment. Do not be put off by the wide range available. I have used Aurifil 12wt in cotton and wool to hand quilt some of the projects, as well as the cotton in the top of my machine when I want my stitches to be more pronounced. Remember, the smaller the number, the thicker the thread. If you are machine stitching with heavier weight threads, remember to use a finer weight in the bobbin. I use Aurifil 40wt in a matching colour whenever I quilt or stitch with their 12wt. You may also need to loosen your top tension slightly. Like fabric, different threads require different needles. If too small a size is used, the thread may fray, shred, or break. For thicker threads, I find a size 100/16 topstitch needle, which has a longer eye and a deeper groove, gives me the best results.

1703 GRASS
GREEN

1263 OLIVE

441 BONSA

480 PICK

1835 BANANA
PEPPER

476 GRELLOW

1677 CURRY

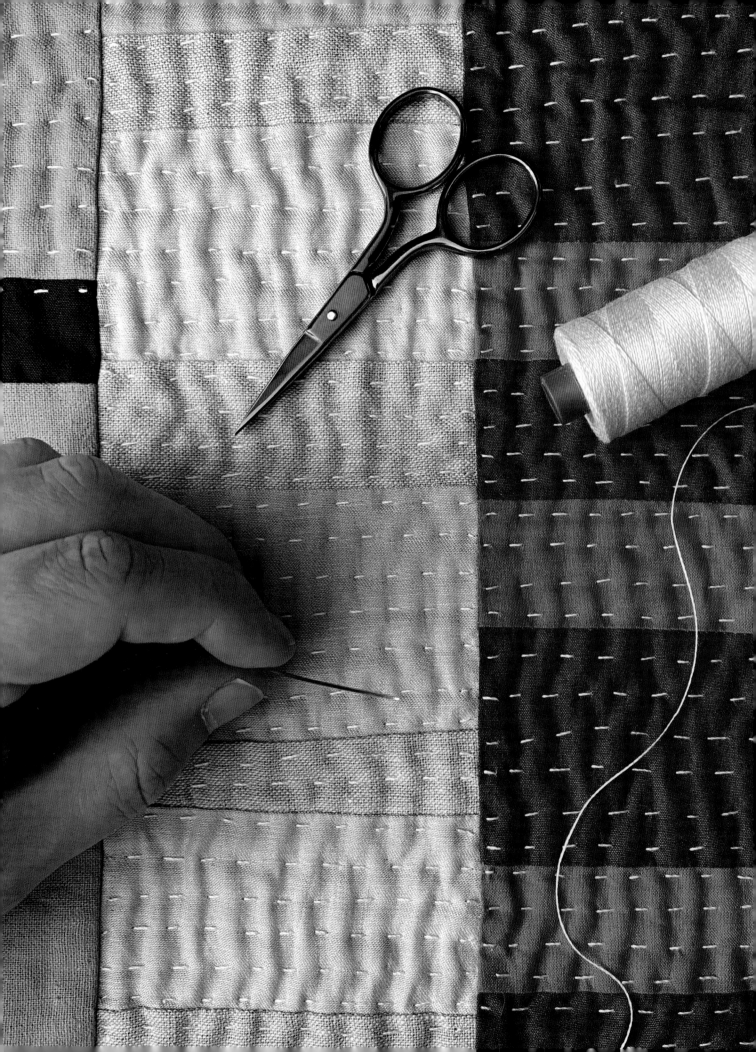

THIMBLE

Perhaps the most divisive sewing notion, the humble thimble provides a barrier between the sewer's fingertip and the blunt end of the needle they are using and has been doing so for centuries. With their usefulness unquestioned, it is their wearability that bring some to dislike them. If, like me, you find thimbles more of a hindrance than a help, you may prefer thimble pads. These are small, self-adhesive discs of leather that stick to your fingertip. Less obtrusive than a thimble, I often forget I'm wearing one. The pad's reusability means I can easily reattach it after a break and get quilting again. A relatively new addition to my sewing room, these have become a must-have, and since I began my foray into hand quilting they offer protection even when quilting heavier weight fabrics, like wool flannel.

HAND QUILTING NEEDLE

Having never hand quilted a quilt before, I quickly discovered that my preferred needle for sewing down bindings and facings wasn't working as well for quilting. The best choice of needle is subjective, though I found a long milliners needle with the largest eye worked well. Trial a few to find one that suits you best.

WOOL PRESSING MAT

Made of compressed wool, these mats offer a firm pressing surface which helps make patchwork seams very flat. As wool's natural structure makes it an efficient insulator, the heat from the iron is retained, so fabric is essentially pressed from both sides. The range of sizes means I can have a smaller one next to my machine. Used alongside a mini iron and a small cutting mat, this set-up is perfect for sewing, cutting, and pressing in one smooth movement. Perfect for someone with my level of impatience!

BONDAWEB OR FUSIBLE WEB

A very popular product for appliqué, fusible web is used to adhere two pieces of fabric together using heat. This is a different product to fusible interfacing or stabiliser (see overleaf) and helps to hold small shapes in place as they are stitched down. There are various weights available and I would always advise using the lightest you can find when sewing stuffed appliqués. Please be sure to follow the manufacturer's instructions carefully.

STABILISER

Commonly used for machine embroidery, stabilisers support the fabric and prevent distortion. Their use is also recommended when stitching any of the decorative stitches your machine may have, especially on fine fabrics. I use a lightweight stabiliser underneath my background fabric whenever I stitch my appliqué shapes down. Look for either a tear-away or cut-away type, rather than fusible, which is permanently adhered to the fabrics. A little goes a long way and you need only cut a piece large enough to cover the area of the fabric shape. Once the appliqué is stitched, the stabiliser is carefully removed.

EMBROIDERY HOOP

Stuffed appliqués are more easily filled when they are under tension. I use a 4" wooden embroidery hoop for this, since my shapes are often small. The hoop size you use should be relative to the size of your appliqué. If you have several shapes stitched to a larger background, a larger diameter hoop will allow you to stuff several shapes at once, rather than moving a smaller hoop around the piece.

FIBRE FILL

Also called toy stuffing, it is this which will give your stuffed appliqués their pronounced appearance. Many brands and types are available, including polyester, which is the most common, cotton, and wool. Polyester is the lightest and won't weigh your project down too much. I recommend buying the best you can afford, as cheaper versions tend to clump more and are not so easy to evenly distribute. As a thriftier alternative, you could use offcuts of wadding cut up into very small pieces, though the result would not be as smooth.

TWEEZERS

A long, thin pair of tweezers will help you stuff the more hard-to-reach parts of your appliqué shapes. Haemostats or surgical forceps with locking jaws grip the stuffing. They also double up as a useful tool for turning out fabric.

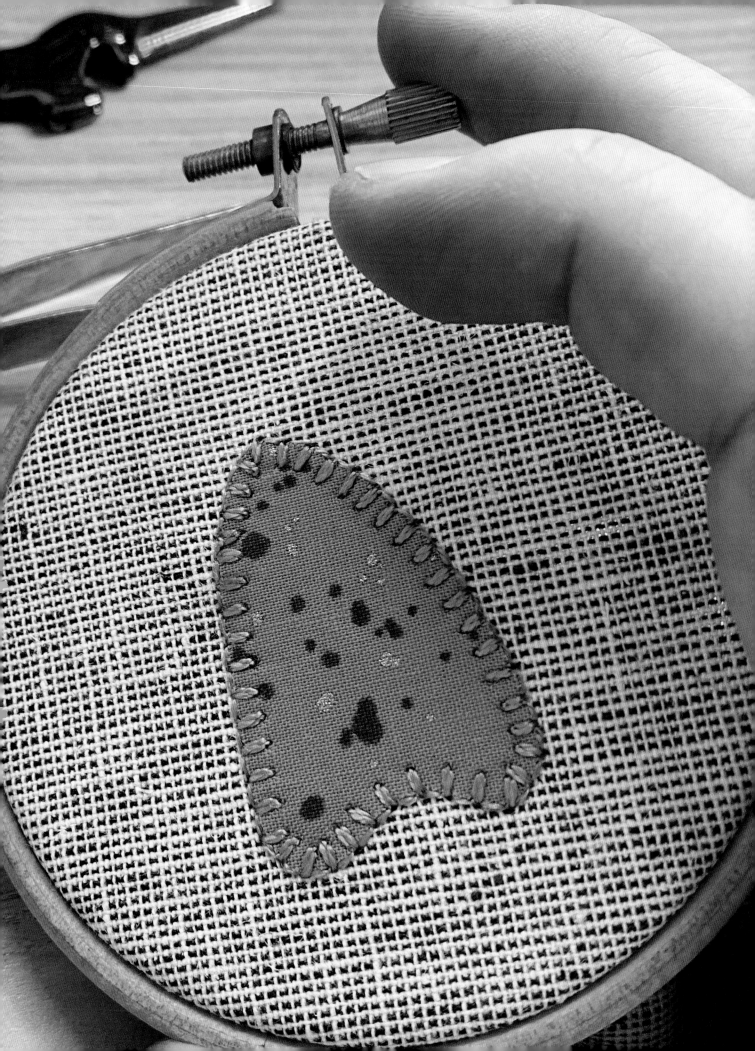

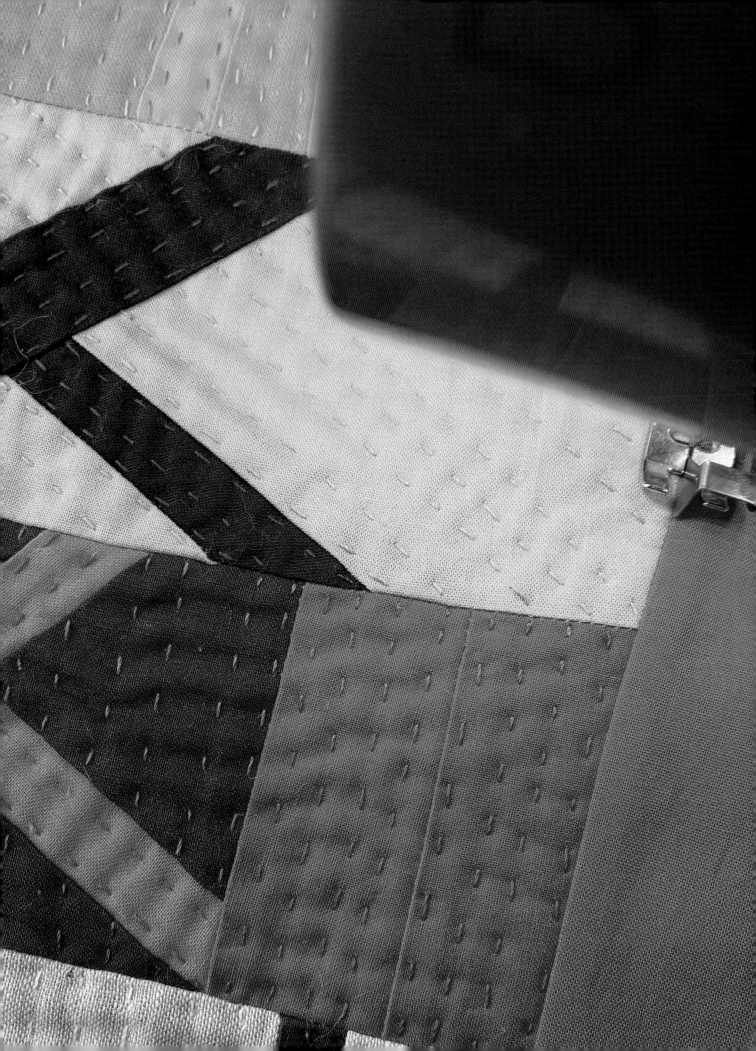

FRAY CHECK

This colourless liquid strengthens and binds fabric. I use a few
drops on the back of my stuffed appliqués to secure the edges
of the stuffing hole after it has been sewn closed. If you are using
loose weave fabric, it will help prevent the fibres from fraying.
The liquid stiffens fabric slightly, so be sure to use only a very small
amount if applying it to any visible parts of your quilt, and test on an
inconspicuous area first.

CUT-OUT RULER

After my appliqué units were stuffed, they were all trimmed to the
same size ready for joining. This task was made easier by a hack to
a spare 6" square ruler I had. Obviously, I wouldn't be able to use the
ruler in its original form, since it would never lay flat on top of the
raised appliqués. To make this possible, I marked a square the size of
my largest shape on the ruler and cut this out using a fine hacksaw,
first carefully drilling a small hole in one corner of the square to give
me a starting point. Once cut out, the resulting aperture could then
be placed over the raised fabric and the block trimmed using the
outer edge of the ruler.

EDGESTITCH OR STITCH IN THE DITCH PRESSER FOOT

This specialist presser foot has a metal bar than runs through the
centre. The bar can be used to aid stitching in the ditch, or can be
butted up against seams and folds of fabric for accurate top or
edgestitching. When attaching facing, a line of edgestitching helps the
facing fold back when it is pressed. When using my Bernina sewing
machine, I move the needle position to the right until the stitching line
is approximately 1/8" from the seam. Each machine will vary, so be
sure to test yours on a practice piece first.

THE PROJECTS

A QUILT THAT CELEBRATES THE PROCESS

CONFETTI and STREAMERS

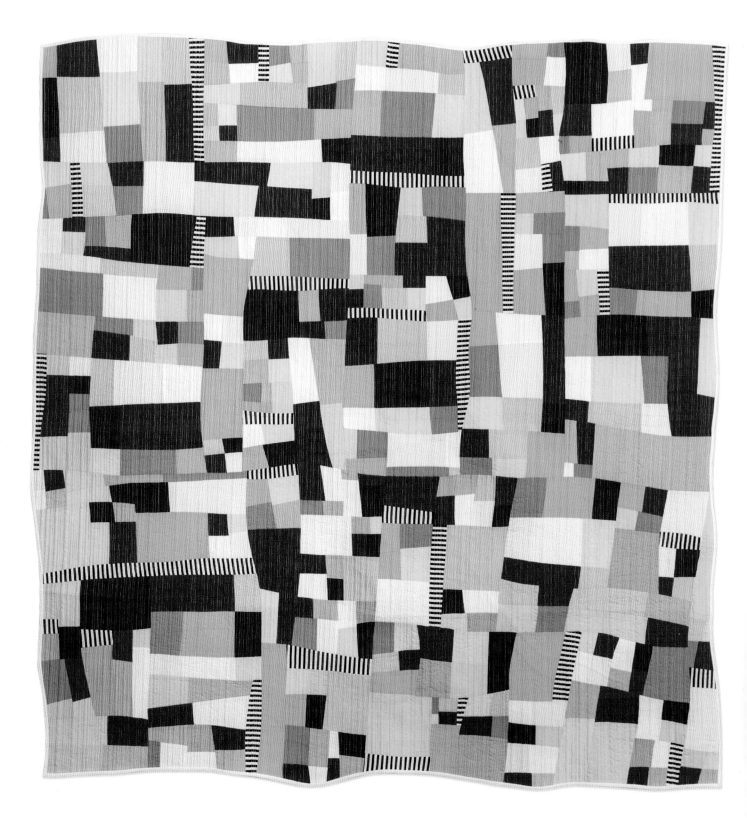

55" X 54"

BEHIND THE SEAMS

Sometimes I like to create a quilt for no other reason than to enjoy the process of making. Whilst quilts can have all kinds of meaning assigned to them, there are moments when the simple pleasure of joining fabric together in a spontaneous way speaks far louder than any other message. It is this sentiment I wanted to capture in this quilt.

From the outset of writing, I knew there had to be at least one project in this book that simply celebrates what we do. It was important to me that the reader understands that sometimes, despite the many different reasons for making an improv quilt, there are occasions when the end result need be nothing more than an object of joy. Of course, one could still find subtle meanings in the creation of such a piece. Whilst there may not be any grand sentiment here, the story told by these stitches celebrates my love of fabric, of colour play and pattern, of line and shape, and of whiling away a few hours whilst the rest of the house sleeps, smiling at the conversations created as each seam is sewn.

Use this idea as an opportunity to challenge your perceptions about how a quilt should be made. When I was making my version, my random playlist offered up Madonna's 'Into the Groove'. A more appropriate soundtrack to make this quilt to there could not be. Removing the reins of a precise pattern will challenge you as a quilter. How to embrace that challenge will vary among quilters and their comfortableness with improvising. If you find yourself stuck, dance for inspiration!

Most importantly, making an improvised quilt does not have to lead to a mutually exclusive relationship. Whilst you may get hooked and never again piece in a traditional way, feel free to flit between both methods. A pattern composed of accurate shapes challenges the brain in a different way and many quilters crave the precision that exact cutting provides. If you ever find yourself overwhelmed or losing interest in a traditionally pieced quilt, then making another in a more liberated way can act as a creative respite, allowing you to reset and recharge before returning to the project.

THE TECHNIQUE

UNPLANNED STACKS

This quilt represents all that I love about improv piecing: the spontaneity, the journey of creating without a fixed plan, and the importance of being open to a change of direction. To help create units more quickly, I've used a stacked technique first explored in 'Inspiring Improv'. For this quilt, the piecing becomes even more organic, since the units are neither created from stacks of the same size nor trimmed to the same dimensions. By taking the technique further and piecing the irregular units together in a jigsaw fashion, you avoid a regimented, blockish layout.

First and foremost, enjoy making the units. Connect with the process and lose yourself in the piecing. Once you have a healthy pile to work with, then you can begin to think about their positions within the finished quilt.

Don't feel that you have to have specific fabrics or measurements to start a quilt like this. Mine was born out of the love of this colour palette. You may have lots of scraps of similar sizes, or perhaps a fat quarter bundle that you've been waiting for the right project to use. Solids naturally lend a cleanness to quilts that I find works so well for this technique. I often prefer to have patterns and shapes emerge from the intersections of the individual pieces meeting, rather than from a print fabric. The addition of a 'zinger' fabric, such as the black and white stripe, adds interest without overwhelming the piece. Used sparingly, it draws the eye around the composition and further adds to the interaction between the seams.

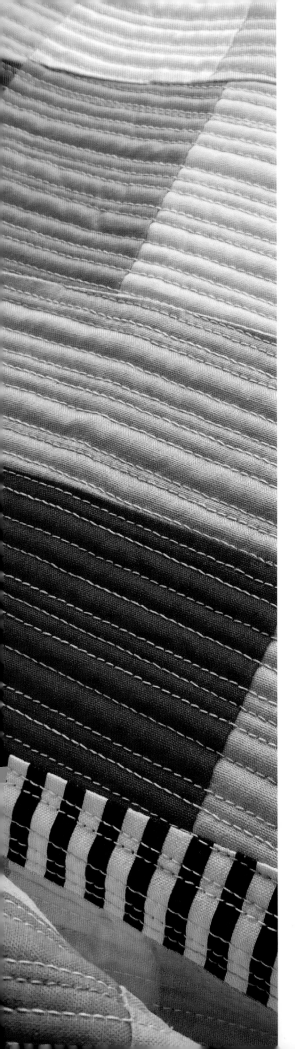

MATERIALS

An assortment of fabric scraps in your chosen colour scheme, in a range of sizes. I used a total of approximately 2 yards of fabric, cut from 12 different solids.

Scraps of a contrasting 'zinger' fabric. This can be a print or high-contrasting colour.

MAKING THE STACKED UNITS

1. Cut four similar sized pieces and layer them right sides up. These pieces do not have to be perfectly square or even straight. What is important is that they are roughly the same size.

2. Make a cut through the stack from one edge to the opposite edge. Vary the angle of this cut with each set of units you make.

3. Take the topmost piece of the right-hand stack and move it to the bottom.

4. Sew the pieces together, press and re-stack them, taking care to keep them in their original order.

5. Make a second cut perpendicular to the first, again adding interest with angular or wonky cuts. Take the top two pieces of the right-hand stack and move them to the bottom. Sew the pieces together and press.

6. Repeat the process using another stack of fabric to create a variety of four-patch units. You can layer more than four pieces of fabric in a stack to create units with varying amounts of shapes in them.

Fig a

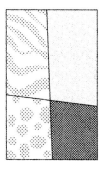 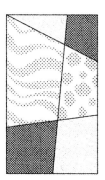 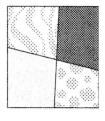

a

PIECING THE QUILT TOP

The different sized stacked units produced by this technique are the building blocks of your quilt. The fun now comes from arranging them into a pleasing composition, remembering that this process is not as easy as when you trim blocks to a uniform size. However, neither is it unachievable; it is simply a different type of challenge. Use the following to help bring energy to your composition.

• Avoid using your ruler exclusively to straighten up the edges. Use scissors sometimes to ensure a not-so-straight seam. Coupling this with straighter seams will help to emphasise their wonkiness.

• Use your iron as something more than just a tool to press. Moving the iron across your seams can add slight distortion which subtly adds to the liberated look of this quilt.

• Bring intent to your work through placement of colour. Fight the urge to not place the same fabrics next to each other. Some of the most interesting shapes are created in this way.

• Once you have several larger slabs, these can then be joined together. Use your zinger fabric as randomly placed sashing, adding to some of the units, but not all. Similarly, alter the size of some of your four-patch units by adding additional fabric to any or all of the sides. *Fig b*

• Avoid the need to have a perfectly straight quilt edge. This idea stems from traditional piecing. Let the outer edges of your stacked units guide you and don't be afraid to trim your quilt into an irregular shape.

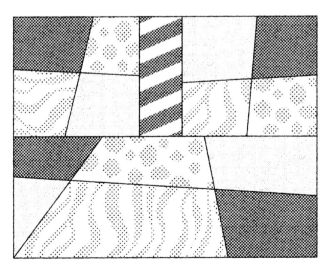

QUILTING NOTES

Whenever I want the piecing to be the focal point of a quilt, I choose a quilting treatment that provides interest not through the colour of the thread or the definition of the stitch, but rather through texture. This texture often comes from dense matchstick quilting. To achieve this on a domestic sewing machine, first ensure that your quilt sandwich is well-basted. Begin by laying down some foundation stitching to secure the layers together. Starting in the middle of the quilt and working out to the edge, stitch lines approximately 3" apart before going back to the middle and stitching in the opposite direction. You can then add additional lines in-between these until the quilting is as dense as you like. Remember, the lines do not have to be perfectly straight.

A QUILT THAT BRINGS PEOPLE TOGETHER

QUILTED BY TRUDI WOOD
49" X 49"

BEHIND THE SEAMS

It's funny how you get used to something. Things
become normal and often, as a consequence, get taken
for granted. Meeting a friend for coffee, visiting your favourite
museum, or travelling to a new city; simple, commonplace pleasures that I'd wager most people
reading this now have a greater appreciation for. Of all the things the COVID-19 pandemic affected, it was
perhaps the lack of human contact and social interaction that hit most people the hardest.

As the latter months of 2019 ticked by, I looked excitedly to the new year and the many social events I
had planned. As well as various workshops and talks, including a teaching trip to Switzerland, my year
was filled with quilt shows, music concerts, and a holiday to France. Many had been organised months
before and eagerly marked in bold ink on the calendar that hung next to my desk. After the buzz of

In March 2020, as the UK entered its first national lockdown, I was wrapping up my Improv Triangle Sewalong, a four-week project I hosted on Instagram, during which I shared my technique for making improv triangles and talked about colour, fabric, and composition. There were participants from all over the world and it was wonderful to see so many different types of quilters connecting with likeminded people, swapping tips, tricks, and inspiration. As 2021 came and the pandemic situation continued to disrupt everyday life, I wanted to host another sewalong as a way to brighten up the gloomy shadow still being cast by COVID-19 and to give people something to channel their energy into. Of all the projects from 'Inspiring Improv', Shoal is the one I have seen people take to the most. When it came to deciding the theme of this new sewalong, the answer was obvious. I was excited to once again connect with a wider audience of quilters, particularly knowing how little social interaction there had been over the course of the past twelve months. The idea of a shoal, a community of quilters with a shared creative goal, seemed like the perfect tonic.

Before the sewalong, I had transitioned to teaching workshops online through Zoom. At first, I wasn't sure how I felt about teaching this way. I loved the vitality of classroom and the shouts of joy I would hear as students realised that, despite their initial doubts, they could work in an improvised way. It was always a pleasure to see their faces when things fell into place. After a few online classes, my doubts were assuaged. Creativity fuels friendship and despite the distance, people made real connections, holding up their work to the screen and championing each other with words of encouragement. Those who lived on the other

side of the world were able to take a class with me from the comfort of their own home and become inspired by a new community of sewers. One such sewer is Melanie Reed, who has attended many of my online workshops. I was interested in hearing how she felt about online teaching and what she took from participating in the Shoal Sewalong.

"Crafting socially has always been a massive part of my life and I hadn't really done much online, except the odd video tutorial on YouTube. When the pandemic hit, I was so grateful for the opportunity to have classes delivered live, especially by such friendly and modern tutors. It's actually been the best of both worlds; interactivity alongside being in your own space, where you have everything you need to hand."

"The quilting community for me has grown and grown with the adaptations to live, online classes. I can be crafting with some of my best local friends and new, interesting people from all over the world! It's been a privilege to do this during some really odd and trying times and it really helped to keep going and keep up the creative endorphins."

"I've participated in a few fun sewalongs that have really kept my focus and my sewing life purposeful, by having an end date in mind. I love the way a sewalong sets a time frame to plan and start sewing, share progress, then crack on to a finish! The improv techniques I've learnt just give me so much more freedom and the people in the sewalong communities really do give each other inspiration. I've loved seeing ideas come to life in fabric. Sharing progress means we all have an opportunity to try out the ideas of others to create our own versions."

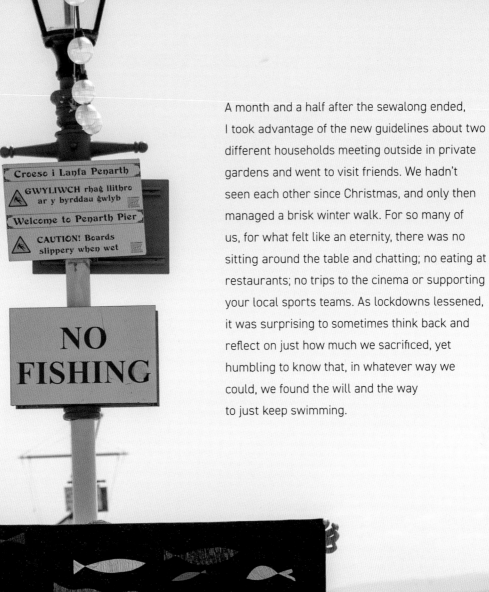

A month and a half after the sewalong ended,
I took advantage of the new guidelines about two
different households meeting outside in private
gardens and went to visit friends. We hadn't
seen each other since Christmas, and only then
managed a brisk winter walk. For so many of
us, for what felt like an eternity, there was no
sitting around the table and chatting; no eating at
restaurants; no trips to the cinema or supporting
your local sports teams. As lockdowns lessened,
it was surprising to sometimes think back and
reflect on just how much we sacrificed, yet
humbling to know that, in whatever way we
could, we found the will and the way
to just keep swimming.

Family: CHARACIDAE

Paracheirodon
Neon Tetra
- **Distribution:** North...
America: Upper Amazo...
- **Length:** Up to 40mm(1...
- **Tank length:** 30cm(12in...
- **Diet:** Worms, small insec...
crustaceans, plant matter an...
dried food.
- **Water temperature:** ...°C
(70-79°F).
- **Compatibility:** Ideal for the
smaller community aquarium but
not with larger fishes.

Until the Cardinal Tetra came
along, the Neon Tetra reigned
supreme as the most colourful
small tetra. It is said to have been
banned from competitive shows
after its introduction to the hobby
in the 1930s because
had an unfair advant...
the rest of the exhib...
to-date story is th...
these fishes are
commercially i...
they are beco...
as Hong K...

Family: CHARACIDAE

Nematobrycon palmeri
Emperor Tetra
- **Distribution:**
An...
Abo...

THE TECHNIQUE

FURTHER FISH

The fish featured in 'Inspiring Improv' were born of a need to showcase both my triangle and freehand curve techniques. My initial inspiration came from childhood drawings of fish which, although not the most detailed, were instantly recognisable despite their simplicity. For my Shoal Sewalong project, I wanted to challenge myself to create more elaborate fish, whilst still maintaining an improvised look. This meant no templates, foundation paper piecing, or measuring.

I expanded on the fish unit's basic construction by varying the tail construction, adding extra fins and gills, and attempting to create some other ocean dwellers. My fabric pull for this quilt was inspired by fish of the black waters of the deep sea, which are often neon bright with bioluminescence. You can make your fish any colour you like and use the variations below to create unique species to populate your quilt.

For my background, rather than the scrappy approach I used for my original Shoal quilt, I used the same fabric throughout, creating a sea of black water to make the vibrant colours of the fish pop.

MATERIALS

An assortment of large scraps in your chosen fish colours. I used a total of approximately 1 yard of fabric.

An assortment of large scraps for the background, either all different for a scrappy look or cut from the same fabric for more cohesiveness. I used a total of approximately 1½ yards of fabric.

Smaller scraps in contrasting or complementary colours for fins, tail inserts, gills, and other details.

QUILTING NOTES

It will come as no surprise that once again I've favoured a dense quilting treatment for this quilt. Whilst the waters of the deep sea are eerily still, they can be quickly stirred into a frenzy by a nightmarish predator closing in on some unsuspecting prey. Alongside narrow matchstick quilting, organic swirls cut through the fish to suggest their movement through the water.

MAKING A BASIC FISH TAIL

This method differs slightly from the triangle technique featured in 'Inspiring Improv' and can be used whether you have solid or patterned background fabric. Using this method, you will be cutting both sides of the background fabric first. Once you are confident in their construction, add variation to your tails using my examples as a starting point.

1. Place a triangle cut from your fish fabric onto a larger square/rectangle of your background fabric, right sides up and aligned along the bottom edge. Ensure there is at least ½" extra background fabric around the triangle.

2. Place your ruler along the left-edge of the triangle and cut through the background fabric, from the lower edge to the top edge. Shift the left background piece out of the way (so as not to trim the tip off accidentally) and cut the right-background piece, once again aligning your ruler along the triangle's edge.

3. Remove the background fabric from beneath the triangle (this can be saved for another triangle unit) then flip the triangle over to the right background piece, right sides together and aligning the cut edges. Sew and press towards the triangle fabric.

4. Trim the dog ear from this sewn section, then place the second background piece, right sides together, aligning it along the remaining edge of the triangle. Sew and press towards the background fabric.

MAKING A BASIC FISH BODY

1. Take a rectangle cut from your fish fabric. The length will determine how long the fish is. Take a background strip approximately half an inch longer than the body strip. The width of this strip will determine the depth of the curve. Place the strips right sides up on your cutting mat and overlap the longer edge. The greater the overlap, the deeper the curve you can cut. Starting at the lower edge, carefully cut a freehand curve through both pieces and discard the excess fabric. From the lower edge, the curve should arc to the mid point of the strips, then arc back down towards the top edge. Use the photograph of my quilt for reference.

2. With right sides together, align the very top of the cut edges and sew the curve. Do not try to align the whole of the curve, but rather focus on the first inch or so in front of the needle. Use your hand to make the edge of the top piece meet the edge of the bottom piece. As you stitch, you will find that the bottom piece remains mostly still, whilst the top piece shifts left and right as it is matched to the curve below. If you need to stop, be sure to do so with the needle in the down position. Press the seam, remembering that being vigorous with your iron is encouraged!

3. Repeat for the other side by overlapping a second strip of background fabric and cutting in the curve. The second curve will mirror the first and will cross through the previously sewn seam, resulting in the basic fish shape. Make sure to allow the background fabric to extend past the top and bottom of the body by at least ¼".

FISH VARIATIONS

Whenever I teach workshops or give talks, I always give a disclaimer warning the attendees that I will overuse the word 'variation' and I make no apologies for it. Although by their nature improv quilts are individual, adding variation can elevate a piece. A basic fish unit is the perfect springboard for further creativity. During the Shoal Sewalong, whether for colour combinations or to help decide how their fish should look, I encouraged the participants to look at images of fish and sea creatures for inspiration. As people became more confident, they were soon sharing not only more and more elaborately detailed fish, but also eels, corals, and seaweed. One participant even pieced a sea turtle!

With improv, the only limit is your imagination. The size, shape, and colour of your units, fish or otherwise, can be as individual as you. If you're making your first fabric shoal, I wholeheartedly encourage you to look beyond nature and create fin-tastical fish!

- Trim the lower edge of the triangle using a freehand curve and add a strip of background fabric to create a wavy tail. *Fig a*

- Before cutting the triangle, piece strips into the fabric to create tails with stripes. The same method can be used to create striped bodies. *Fig b-f*

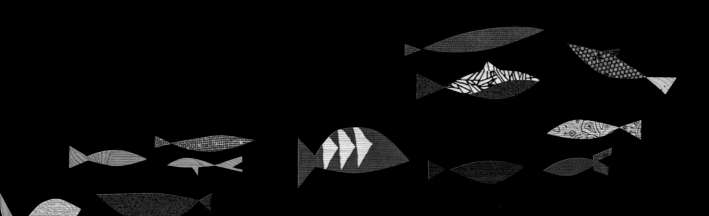

- To create a multi-triangle tail, first make a basic triangle unit. From this, cut a triangle and piece this into background fabric. This can be repeated as many times as you like. Experiment with fabric and colour choice to create some really interesting versions. If the background fabric is used as an inner triangle, a completely different tail shape can be created. *Figs g-h*

- Rather than creating individual triangle units, you can sew multiple triangles in a row. These work really well as fins, spines, or even teeth. First make a basic triangle unit, then cut the angle for your next triangle in the right background piece. Sew a second triangle into place, then add more background fabric to the right of this. Repeat until you reach the required length. With this method, you don't have to have the triangles pre-cut. You can cut the angle into the background fabric, sew a larger scrap of fish fabric to it, then trim the right-hand side. You can either leave a gap between each triangle or overlap them. *Figs i-j*

- Create a wide triangle unit. This can then be used as one of the background strips when you piece the fish body. This is a great way to add fins to the top and bottom of your fish. A longer strip of multiple triangles, as described above, can also be used in this way. *Figs k-l*

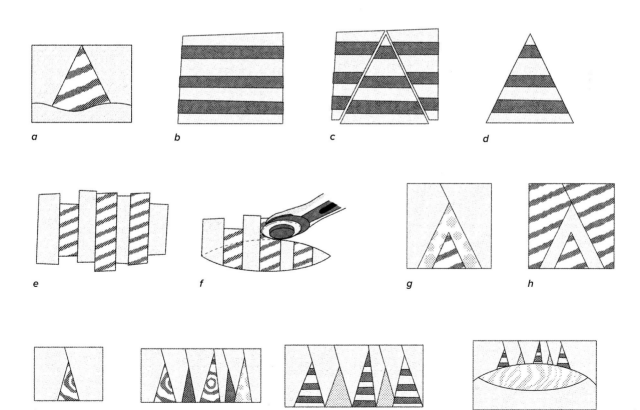

a

b

c

d

e

f

g

h

i

j

k

l

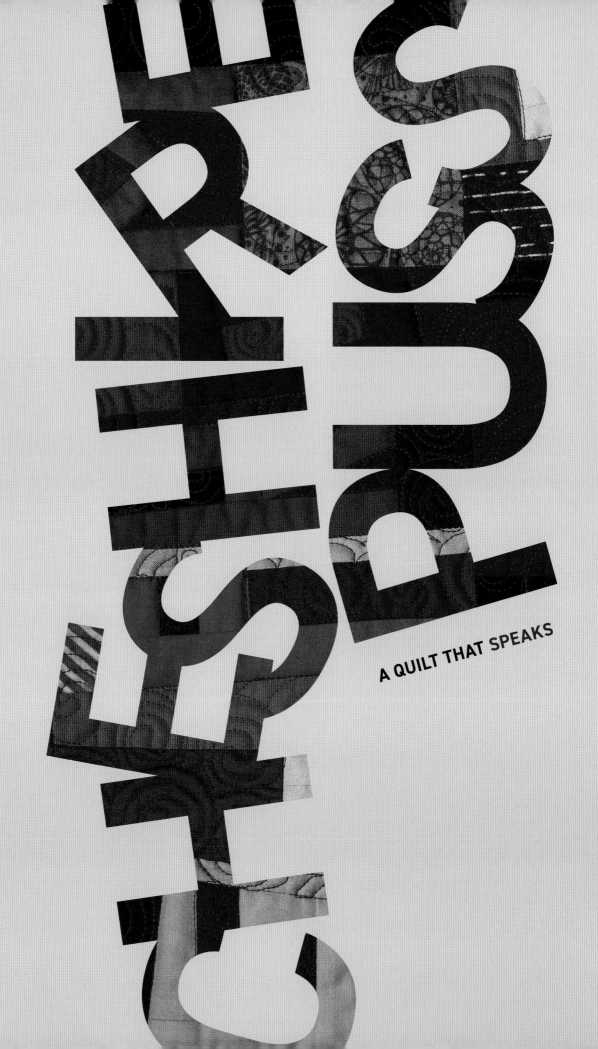

A QUILT THAT SPEAKS

It is a mistake to think that quilts have only

BEHIND THE SEAMS

recently become revolutionary

For centuries, quilters have had a lot to say. Like the poet with his pen, words of support, rebellion, protest, and political resistance have been stitched by sewers upon the blank pages of their quilts. The reasons behind these affirmations vary greatly, yet each was sure to be an emotional outlet for the maker, perhaps a cathartic process to deal with grief, loss, or anger. Throughout history, many of these makers were often marginalised and so used quilts to bring to light the various injustices that pervaded their lives.

During the American Civil War, as well as the utility quilts made to warm Union soldiers on the front line, quilters on both sides of the political divide used fabrics printed with words and slogans in an early nod to activism.

In the collection of the Iolani Palace in Hawaii, Queen Lili'uokalani's quilt, started during her imprisonment after American forces overthrew the Kingdom of Hawaii, proclaims from its centre block "*Imprisoned at Iolani Palace, January 17th 1895...we began this quilt there*". It serves both as an historical marker and reflection of the political climate of the time. On a more personal level, the anguish suffered by its maker is in every stitch.

After the Japanese invasion of Singapore during the Second World War, the notorious Changi Prison housed men, women, and children. Families were separated and communication was strictly forbidden. To let their husbands know they were alive, the women, spurred on by Canadian inmate Ethel Mulvany, made a set of patchwork quilts for the hospital in the military section where the men were housed. Disguised amongst this act of womanly kindness, quilt blocks were stitched with coded messages informing the men that their families were safe.

In 1985, in remembrance of the assassinations of Harvey Milk and George Moscone in 1978, people marched with signs upon which they had written the name of a loved one lost to AIDS-related causes. It was these signs that inspired the largest community art project in the world, the NAMES Project AIDS Memorial. Made up of 48,000 panels, this quilt commemorates hundreds of thousands of lives in quilted, appliquéd, and embroidered words. With new panels being added, the quilt and the legacy of those lost continues to grow. The AIDS Quilt has inspired many other community projects, including the K.I.A Quilt, made to commemorate those killed in active service during the Iraqi War, as well as several quilts which memorialise the victims of the September 11th terrorist attacks.

My first encounter with text quilts was the work of Chawne Kimber, whom I happened upon by chance, as is so often the case these days, when researching text quilts from my contribution to 43 For 43. By positioning them in the public sphere, Chawne's quilts become part of a conversation about race and identity. I was immediately struck by her bold use of text to convey her thoughts and feelings.

Phrases like *"stop the war on women"* and *"you are beautiful"* are pieced into improvised compositions. Most arresting is her Still Not quilt, with the words *"I am still not free"* emblazoned across a patchwork of blue squares. Her NSFW quilts challenge the idea of acceptability in quilt making, accompanied by a disclaimer that advises looking away if you don't appreciate the full use of the English language.

Further research since, has led me to discover a whole array of contemporary makers who have continued to give their quilts a voice. The MQG's QuiltCon in 2018 was particularly affecting, with many entries, some more overt than others, made in response to social and political issues. Feminism, pro-immigration, and the rights of women were some of the topics of conversation. The Viewer's Choice that year was awarded to Liz Harvatine for her stirring piece She Was Warned, inspired by *"Elizabeth Warren and all of the other women who stand up and fight and resist and persist in the United States of America"* and features hand quilting in the penmanship of sixty different American Women.

QUILTED BY TRUDI WOOD
71" × 65"

THE TECHNIQUE

AN IMPROV ALPHABET

For me, the most striking quilts that convey a message are those that feature text, rather than an abstract representation through colour, line, or shape. As you read the words across the surface of the quilt, one cannot belie the intent of the maker.

Letters of a text quilt can be formed in many ways, with appliqué or foundation paper piecing being popular techniques. I wanted to expand upon the improvised way of making letters I first explored in my contribution to 43 For 43. You can use this improv alphabet to create any message you like. For my quilt, I was inspired by one of my favourite passages, taken from Lewis Carroll's 1865 classic 'Alice's Adventures in Wonderland'. Though I have read this work many times, it was in 2012 when the passage took on a special meaning. I was asked to give a small reading at the wedding of a friend. I first met Stacey Pedersen in Paris in 2006. I was immediately struck by her free-spiritedness, her love of travel, and sense of adventure. This quote perfectly summed up her willingness to find adventure in all places and to take enjoyment from the journey, rather than the destination.

"Would you tell me, please, which way I ought to go from here?"

"That depends a good deal on where you want to get to," said the Cat.

"I don't much care where -" said Alice.

"Then it doesn't matter which way you go," said the Cat.

"- so long as I get somewhere." Alice added as an explanation.

"Oh, you're sure to do that," said the Cat, "if you only walk long enough."

Though not as well-known as other quotes from the book, this exchange between Alice and the Cheshire Cat perfectly sums up the improvised way of sewing.

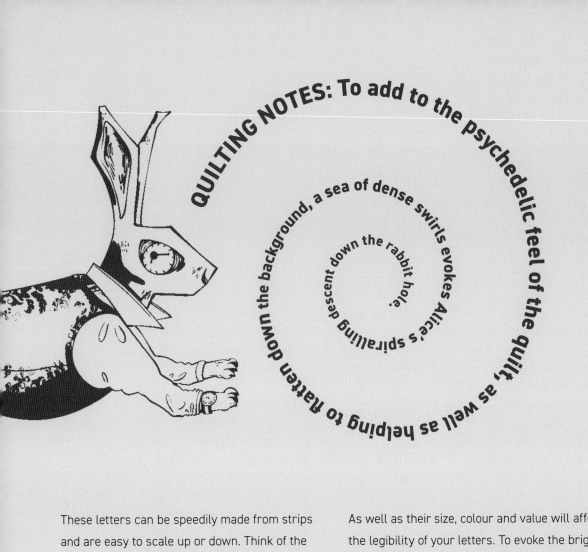

QUILTING NOTES: To add to the psychedelic feel of the quilt, as well as helping to flatten down the background, a sea of dense swirls evokes Alice's spiralling descent down the rabbit hole.

These letters can be speedily made from strips and are easy to scale up or down. Think of the width of the initial strips as your chosen writing implement; if you want narrow letters, as if they were written by a fine fountain pen, then your strips should be narrow. For big, bold letters, like those penned in a permanent marker, use wider strips. I found it easier to make letters first, then piece those into words and sentences. You can work in rows, as I have done, or position your text in a more random arrangement. You can add variation to the letters by using a mixture of strip widths, using a scrappy background, and making slight changes to the way some letters are formed. When joining them into sentences, be sure to read twice, sew once. Failure on my part to do so almost resulted in a misquote.

As well as their size, colour and value will affect the legibility of your letters. To evoke the bright, topsy-turvy world Carroll created, I chose a saturated colour scheme, purposely including letters made from fabric similar in colour to the background they were set in. I wanted the viewer to stumble upon words, to perhaps need a second or third glance to decipher them. Use the following instructions more like a recipe rather than a blueprint, so that your letters are all a little different, just like your handwriting, and easily adaptable to suit the message you want to convey. Though you might not know exactly where you're going when you set off, you're sure to reach a destination and be challenged creatively along the pathway to it.

MATERIALS

WOF strips in your chosen text fabric. These should be cut to the width you want your letters to be, plus ½″ for the seam allowance. I used a total of approximately 1 yard of fabric, cut from 22 different coloured solids.

Background pieces. I opted for a scrappy background and used a total of approximately 1½ yards of fabric.

MAKING THE LETTERS

Using the illustrations as a guide, cut pieces from your text fabric and background fabric, matching the basic shapes that form the letter and remembering to make them bigger or smaller to suit the size you wish to make. I use scissors for this, offering up the letter strip to the background piece and roughly cutting to the required length, whilst ensuring I leave a slight overhang at each end. Lay the pieces out on your cutting mat to form the letter.

Following the sewing order, stitch the letter together piece by piece, pressing each seam and trimming any excess as you go. Depending on the scale of your letters and the width of the strips, you may need to take a looser approach with your pressing and alternate between open and to-the-side. Fabric pressing spray will help flatten any particularly bulky seams.

Once sewn, letters can be joined into words with or without a narrow strip between them. You can also add fabric to any or all sides to make them bigger.

Add variation to the letters by using a scrappy background. You can also make the strips of the letters wider at one end, shorten the strokes of some letters by adding a small piece of background fabric, and use half-square triangles for the centres of letters such as B, O, and Q, etc. For the punctuation, if several are needed, it is quicker to strip piece a longer section and sub-cut it.

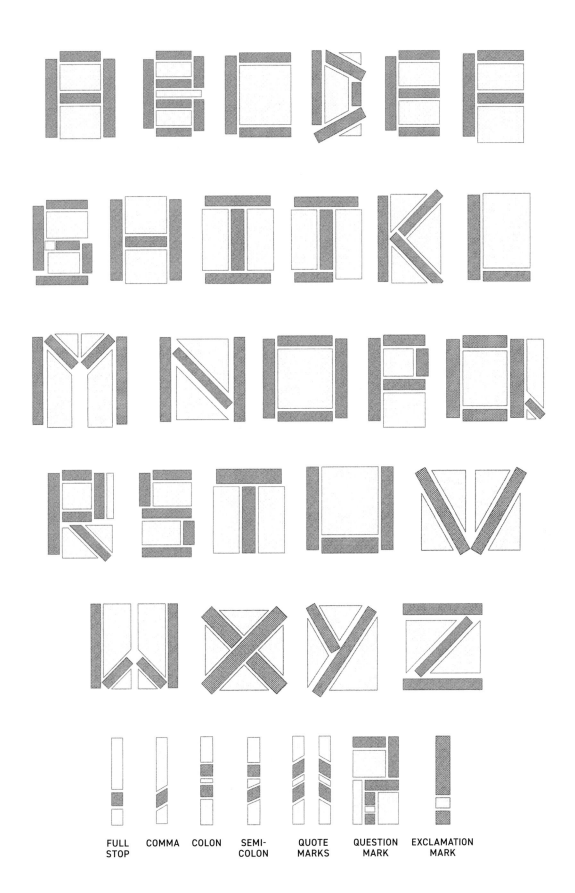

FULL
STOP

COMMA

COLON

SEMI-
COLON

QUOTE
MARKS

QUESTION
MARK

EXCLAMATION
MARK

THE PATH HAS NEVER BEEN EASY

BEHIND THE SEAMS

2020 was a year of awakening. For me, as a white person, it was the year that revealed something which I had shamefully been blind to for far too long. I know that I live my life from a position of privilege. What I've come to understand is that this privilege often clouds my view of what other, more marginalised members of society may be facing. For some, these obstacles are a daily occurrence. Simple things that I take for granted are invariably different or more difficult for others solely because of their skin colour: access to health care, jobs, and housing.

In normal circumstances, I would never have heard the name George Floyd. It should have been just like the other eight billion names that make up the global population: unknown and meaningless. Yet in May 2020 it was chanted by protesters seeking justice after he was murdered by Derek Chauvin, a white Minneapolis police officer who, despite Floyd being handcuffed and lying face down, knelt on his neck for over nine minutes. In a woeful repeat of history, the words *"I can't breathe"*, the last of Eric Garner and spoken eleven times before he was killed by a NYPD officer in 2014, were once more uttered by an African American prior to dying.

In the weeks and months that followed, set against a backdrop of the ongoing COVID-19 pandemic, thousands of people gathered to seek justice for Floyd, first in the United States, followed shortly after by many other countries. Protestors were unified in their opposition to racism, police brutality, and the arming of America's police force. This expression of solidarity awoke in me a desire to better understand the unjust society we live in. I had never before witnessed the deadly failings of a police system, whose role it is to protect and serve, so viscerally played out, despite reports by 'The New York Times' which state over 70 people who have died in police custody had uttered the words *"I can't breathe"*.

I realised that I had been colourblind, which prevented me from seeing what atrocities were taking place. I needed to do better. The onus was on me to educate myself and remove the blinkers. I was not prepared for what I learnt. Javier Ambler, Elijah McClain, Breonna Taylor, Michael Brown; so many cases of police brutality that I was not aware of. I was frustrated at myself and the broken system of which I was a part. I began asking myself many questions.

Do I engage in behaviours that are harmful to people of colour? What can I do to demonstrate my solidarity to these people and their efforts towards equality? I read more about race. I listened to people of colour speak about their experiences. I sought out black makers and engaged more with their work. Even in my own community, I was shocked to discover the racism experienced by black makers. I was too used to hearing the experiences of people who look like me.

My journey of education led me to discover the Social Justice Sewing Academy - a collective of intergenerational textile artists founded by Sara Trail, who use their work to express how they feel about various social issues faced in their community and engender support. Following the death of Trayvon Martin, a 17-year old African-American from Florida, in 2017, Sara, an active member of the quilting community, was disturbed by the lack of action in response to the tragedy and channeled her frustration into a portrait quilt to honour Martin.

In 2020 the Social Justice Sewing Academy was founded to raise awareness about systemic racism. Their quilts help to foster conversations not only about the Black Lives Matter movement, but also women's rights, LGBTQ+ equality, gun

reform, and immigration. Their work has been exhibited at QuiltCon, as well as at many other museums and art venues across the United States. In 2021, 'Stitching Stolen Lives', co-written with Sara by Teresa Duryea Wong, was published. This moving book takes an in-depth look at the Social Justice Sewing Academy's Remembrance Project and showcases quilts and banners which not only memorialise lost individuals, but give voice to their young makers.

This new generation of artivisim inspired me to channel my own feelings into something familiar and acknowledge my new-found understanding. I wanted to make a quilt that depicted the uneven playing field that dominates our society. I used strips of fabric to represent two pathways. Starting at the top left, these span the surface of the quilt to reach the lower left edge. By taking the white path, this point can be reached quicker and more easily than the black, which turns and presents dead ends. When taking the black path, there is only one way to reach the final destination: the long way. Making this quilt allowed for moments of reflection about society and my place in it. Though I have much more work to do, I reflect upon the words of Maya Angelou, who said "*I did then what I knew how to do. Now that I know, I do better*".

MICHELLE "TAMIKA" WASHINGTON
LACI HESS, 2020

JESSICA HERNANDEZ
REBECCA GRECO 2020

SUSTAINABILITY COMMUNITY QUILT
VARIOUS STUDENTS FROM SSJA WORKSHOPS,
EMBROIDERED BY SSJA VOLUNTEERS, PIECED BY EASY
BAY HERITAGE QUILTERS, QUILTED BY NANCY WILLIAMS

QUILTED BY TRUDI WOOD
35" X 26"

THE TECHNIQUE

QUILT FACING

Since it was important that the path defined by the black fabric strips entered and exited at the sides of the quilt, I didn't want to finish it with a binding, which would enclose the composition and be distracting. By using a facing, the patchwork and quilting extend to the very edges of the quilt and allows the eye to trace the uninterrupted line that forms part of the story. Facings lend themselves to quilts that are intended to be hung, rather than used, and give a more artful finish.

Like binding, different quilters will have different methods for sewing facings. I use the following technique for both straight and curved edges, though I do not take the time to cut bias strips for curved edges. In fact, all the curved quilts I have made, whether they have been bound or faced, were finished using straight grain strips. I find that a little persuasion and some gentle tugging can make the strip fit even the most voluptuous curve. This method also needs angular corners. For rounded corners, circular quilts, or quilts with entirely curved edges, use the bagged-out method.

When facing a quilt, I match the facing fabric to the quilt backing, which gives a minimal, cohesive look. The successfulness of a facing relies on good pressing, ensuring that the strips are not visible from the front of the quilt. You may prefer to choose a fabric that blends with the outer edges of the quilt top, which will make any not-quite-perfect pressing less visible.

When calculating the length of the facing strips for straight edge quilts, measure one side of your quilt and add 4". Cut a 2" wide strip this length. Repeat for the other three sides of the quilt, remembering which strips go where if the edges of the quilt are all different lengths. For curved edged quilts, use a wider 3" strip.

MATERIALS

4 strips of facing fabric, cut to length as instructed on page 173.

PREPARING THE FACING STRIPS

Press the long edge of each strip over by ¼". If you are using a print, press to the wrong side. *Fig a*

FACING THE QUILT

1. Trim your quilt so that the backing and wadding are even with the edges of the quilt top. *Fig b*

2. Place your quilt right side up and position a facing strip along the top edge of your quilt. The non-folded edge should run parallel along the quilt edge and the fold should be visible (quilt and facing fabric right sides together). There will be an overhang of 2" at each end. *Fig c*

3. Stitch the facing strip to the quilt using a ¼" seam allowance. *Fig d*

4. Press the strip away from the quilt using a really hot iron. Take care not to distort the quilt sandwich seam allowance.

5. Using an edgestitch foot if you have one, position the metal bar along the edge of the pressed strip and stitch as close to the fold as you can along the length of the strip, moving your needle position accordingly. When using your standard presser foot, aim to sew close to the fold. *Fig e*

6. Press the facing strip to the back of the quilt, taking the bulk of the seam allowance to the back too. For curved edges, you will need to work the seam a little more. Be patient and use steam if necessary. *Fig f*

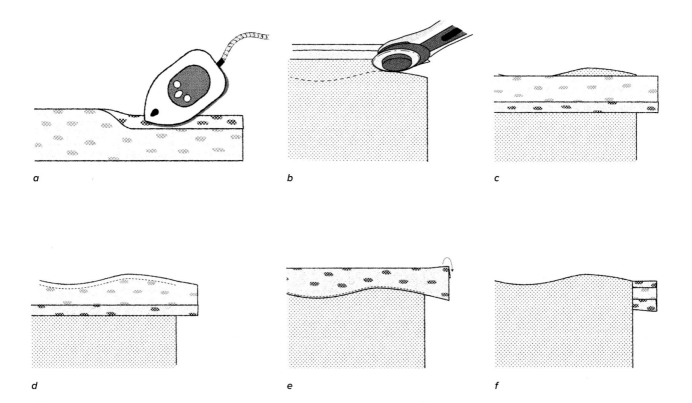

a

b

c

d

e

f

7. Trim the excess from the strip at each end so that the facing is level with the edge of the quilt. Repeat steps 2 - 7 for the bottom edge of the quilt. *Fig g*

8. Follow steps 2 - 7 again to attach, press, edgestitch, and press again the two side facing strips to the quilt. Take care to ensure that the top and bottom strips already attached remain flat. Pin in place if necessary. Do not trim the 2" overhang from these side strips.

9. Fold one side facing strip down, away from the quilt. Then fold in the excess at the end of the strip that you did not trim, so that it is even with the edge of the quilt. Fold the facing strip back up so that the tail is concealed. Repeat for the other end. *Figs h-j*

10. Hand stitch into position using a small slipstitch, using pins if you wish and taking care to avoid the stitches passing through to the front of the quilt. Repeat steps 9 and 10 for the remaining side facing strip. *Fig k*

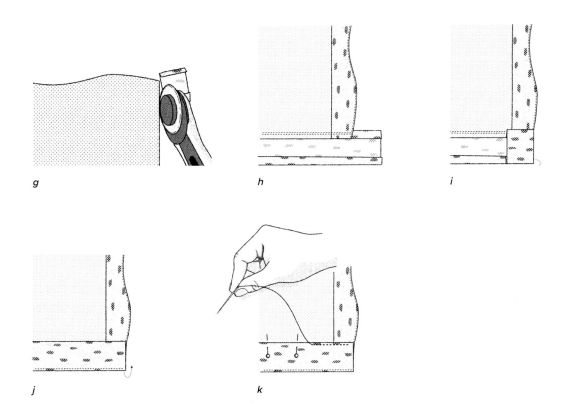

g

h

i

j

k

BAGGED-OUT FACING

MATERIALS

A piece of fabric large enough to cover your whole quilt, plus at least 1" extra around all sides. Depending on the size of your quilt, you may need to join pieces to achieve the width needed. This method places the quilt and facing fabric right sides together. This is particularly important to remember when facing irregularly shaped quilts. Keep in mind that if the facing fabric is right side up when cut to the shape of the quilt, it will not match - it will be reversed.

FACING THE QUILT

1. Trim your quilt so that the backing and wadding are even with the edges of the quilt top.

2. Place the facing fabric right side up, then place the quilt right side down on top of it. Secure the two together using safety pins. Do not pin too close to the edge. If facing a large quilt, pull the facing fabric taut first and secure to a table or the floor using tape.

3. Stitch around the entire perimeter of the quilt using a ¼" seam allowance, taking care with any deep curves or irregular edges.

4. Trim the excess facing fabric to match the quilt edge. Carefully clip the seam allowance of any deep curves, avoiding the stitched line.

5. Flip the quilt over so that the wrong side of the facing fabric is upward. Make a slit in the facing fabric approximately 2½" away from the seam line. Following the perimeter of the quilt, carefully cut away the centre of the facing fabric. You can introduce new shapes here, though be sure to not cut closer than 2" to the seam line. The excess facing fabric can be re-used for another smaller facing or for patchwork.

6. Turn the facing fabric to the back of the quilt. Use a point turner or chopstick to help push out the seam. Press well and ensure the bulk of the seam allowance lies flat.

7. Turn the raw edge of the facing under. The seam allowance of any deep curves can be carefully clipped to help them turn under more easily. Press well and pin into position.

8. Hand stitch the facing down using a small slipstitch, taking care to avoid the stitches passing through to the front of the quilt.

QUILTING NOTES

For this quilt, it was important that the quilting did not distract from the piecing. For that reason, coordinating thread was used to quilt dense lines, following the shapes of the strips and the path they create. A slightly heavier weight thread was used to add more texture to the black sections, suggesting a longer, more arduous route.

A QUILT THAT HONOURS

EVERY CLOUD

BEHIND THE SEAMS

The symbolism of the rainbow is rich and varied. As a child I remember being excited and annoyed in equal measure whenever one would appear. They were fascinating to look at, yet impossibly difficult to get close enough to touch. My friends and I would pedal our bikes ever-faster as we sped towards what we thought must surely be the end, only to discover the rainbow mocking us from the brow of the next hill.

Today, I've come to appreciate the rainbow as more than a symbol of a passing storm or a naive way to memorise colours. Their meaning is much more varied. They represent hope following periods of darkness and loss; their association with good luck stems from Celtic and Irish mythology, inviting many to come seek out the leprechaun's pot of gold rumoured to be buried at the end; Norse mythology and Buddhist teaching

associate the rainbow with the link between life and death, whilst for members of the LGBTQ+ community, the unification of colours seen in various pride flags have represented equality, community, and diversity since the late 1970s.

During the disruptive and uncertain months of the COVID-19 outbreak, the world was at odds. There was disagreement at every level about the best way to tackle the virus. The pandemic brought to light issues of inequality, racial and geographical discrimination, misinformation, health equity, and the exacerbation of political tensions. Whilst governments and world leaders tackled the situation with varying degrees of success, for the average person, what mattered most was the health and safety of loved ones and as speedy a return to normality as possible.

39" X 22"

Despite the differing opinions people may have had about the pandemic and the response to it, the UK was unified by a great appreciation for frontline workers of the NHS, who battled an unseen enemy daily amid terrifying conditions. Everyone agreed that the debt of gratitude owed to not only NHS staff, but to key workers across all sectors, was something that would be hard to repay. As a sign of support and solidarity, rainbows began appearing in house windows, created by children whose schools had been closed. Making them brought a sense of pride to pupils, who thought about the people they might make smile as they walked past the house. Soon rainbows began to appear in cars, on Facebook profiles, and city centre roundabouts. People began to actively seek them out on their walks and many turned to paper craft and paint to decorate their own windows with a small sign of hope. Emblazoned with words of thanks to doctors, nurses, and teachers, rainbows spread across the country, signalling a unified stance of solidarity and support.

Despite the negative impact the pandemic had, there were positives to be found. By being required to stay at home, people returned to a simpler way of living and both discovered and rediscovered passions and pastimes that their previously busy lives may not have allowed. There was a resurgence in baking, with flour and yeast becoming scarce in many supermarkets; people reconnected with nature through gardening, family walks, and bike rides; jigsaws, often viewed as a pastime of the elderly, sold out online; crafts, particularly sewing and knitting, exploded. This renaissance led to a shortage of sewing machines which saw my days at Bernina UK become busier than we had known for a long time. Not since the airing of 'The Great British Sewing Bee' had the public's interest in sewing been so invigorated!

THE TECHNIQUE

CURVED WEDGES

It's not surprising that for the rainbow that hung in our window, I turned to fabric. I joined arcs of colour with freehand curves and set the rainbow into a background of grey linen. The piece was then quilted simply using a walking foot to echo the shapes of the arcs. A curved binding in a narrow black and white stripe framed the piece ready for hanging.

I decided to rework this smaller rainbow quilt into something larger, focusing on the idea of clouds and the silver lining within. I wanted to create a quilt that acknowledged the terrible situation we found ourselves in, yet showed that even in the darkest times of adversity and struggle, there is hope. To piece the cloud sections, I used curved wedges to create the shape. This technique is a useful addition to your improv toolbox and is a way to add curved interest through the use of straight seams. The resulting sections can be quilts in their own right, scaled appropriately to reach the desired finished size, or they can be pieced together as I have, using curved seams. I added a larger section of black fabric to finish the lower edge of the cloud. To create the rainbow lining of the cloud, I used reverse appliqué to add a small section of coloured fabric beneath the cloud.

The curved line is created by sewing wedges together, which are either narrower or wider than each other at their base. The initial size you cut the rectangles will determine the scale of the unit. If you want a large curved unit more quickly, make your starting rectangles larger. Since these rectangles will be trimmed into the wedge shape, feel free to use scissors to cut them. They do not have to be either perfectly straight or exact rectangles. Have fun expressing yourself through these cuts.

Before you start piecing a wedge unit, you may wish to create a reference by drawing the line of the curve you hope to achieve. This may not be necessary if you are being totally spontaneous, yet for me, when trying to create a cloud shape, I found it useful to have something to refer to and keep me roughly on track. You can sketch the shape on paper or use a length of wool or string to plot the line directly onto your design wall. That way, you can check your progress against this line with each new addition you sew.

You are in control of the shape of these units. To curve the shape downwards, make the base narrower; to curve it upwards, slowly make the bases of the subsequent wedges wider. As you continue to add to the unit, you'll feel more confident about the way shapes can be created and even add straighter sections for contrast and interest.

MATERIALS

Strips of fabrics. These can be different widths but should be approximately the same length. I used a total of approximately 1 yard of fabric, from 20 different fabrics, and cut strips approximately 6" long.

QUILTING NOTES

I used hand quilting for parts of this quilt. For the curved cloud sections, I used the same machine quilting treatment as I did for the smaller rainbow, stitching perpendicular lines in a heavier weight thread. For the cloud lining and black base, I used big hand stitching in the same weight thread, to add texture. The rainbow fabric is peppered with stab stitching of various lengths, whilst the black is quilted using organic crosses, meaning that each is slightly different, with no effort made towards uniformity. These represent all the bright lights that shone during the COVID-19 crisis. Lights from medical staff and hospital workers, to teachers, bus drivers, and those involved in food production, distribution and sale.

MAKING THE UNITS

1. Take your first fabric piece and place it on your cutting mat right side up. Take the next piece and overlap the longer edge, again right side up. Cut an angle thorough both layers and discard any excess.

2. Place the two pieces right sides together, aligning the newly cut edges, and sew. Press the seam in your preferred way. *Fig a*

3. Take another rectangle and overlap as above. Again, make an angled cut through both pieces, making the base of the previous wedge wider or narrower, depending on which way you want the unit to curve. Sew and press. *Fig b*

4. Continue to add rectangles in this way, altering the width of the bases until the unit is the required shape or you feel it is finished. As the shape grows, use a really hot iron and some fabric flattening spray to help everything lay flat. Offer up your pieced section to your reference curve often to ensure everything is staying on course. *Fig c*

5. These curved wedge units can be joined together using curved seams. I encourage you to first play with the layout and trial different positions. This part is like a jigsaw and some pieces will fall into place more easily than others. The curved seams are sewn in the same way as the freehand curves used for the improv fish units. Overlap the two sections you are joining right sides up and cut the curve. Remove the excess, then place the pieces right sides together and stitch slowly, easing the fabric edges together as you do. I prefer not to pin, though you can if you wish. Open up the seam and iron vigorously! For particularly expressive curves, once you overlap and cut them, you can make small notches along the seam line which can be matched up when the seam is sewn, similar to the notched markings used in dressmaking. This will help to keep everything where it should be.

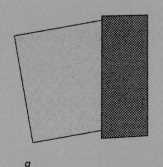

a

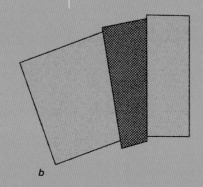

b

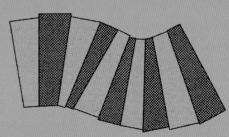

c

Viral Temperature

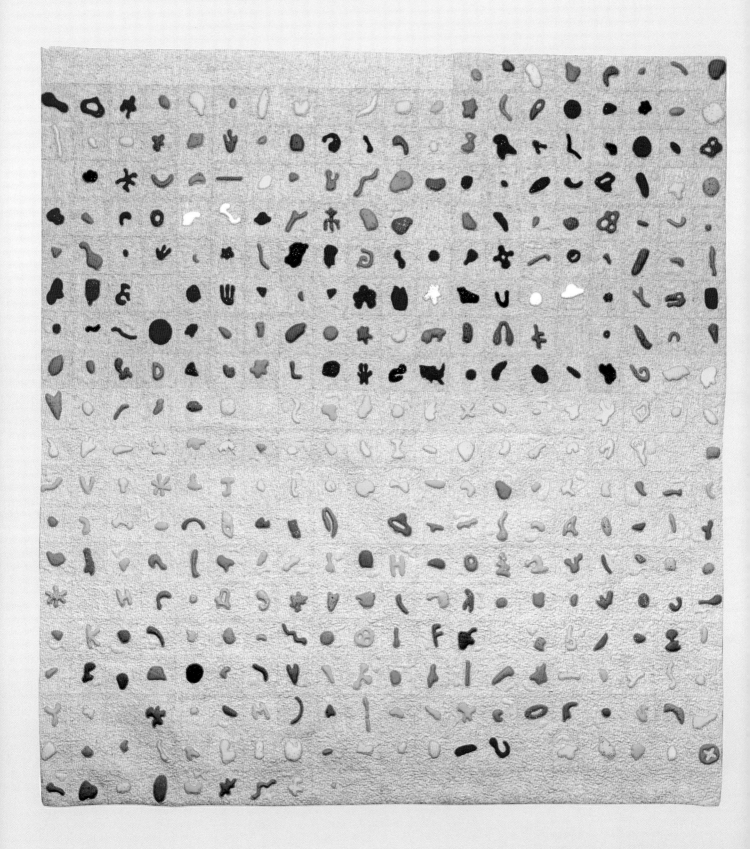

QUILTED BY TRUDI WOOD
59" X 59"

BEHIND THE SEAMS

One of the positives of social media is the opportunity to happen upon work by others which may ignite a creative spark in your own practice. In March 2020, a scroll through my Instagram feed brought my attention to Jo Avery's current work in progress: a temperature quilt. Not for the first time, I was enamoured by her use of fabric as she appliquéd colourful, organically shaped circles to equally vibrant squares.

Using a quilt to record the daily highs and lows of a city or town was something I'd encountered a few examples of during the time I'd been quilting. I'd also seen knitted and crocheted versions, with rows and rows of bright yarns reflecting a scorching summer or a bitterly cold winter.

The concept behind these quilts is simple and often starts by assigning a fabric to a specific temperature or temperature range. After choosing a day to begin, which, surprisingly to some, doesn't have to be the first of January, you record this temperature in the form of a quilt block, with half-square triangles and drunkard's path being just two of the many interpretations. Repeat 364 times and you have a visual record of your location's yearly temperature range. Some quilters record either the high or low temperature, whilst others record both. Some introduce meteorological aspects into their quilts and choose creative ways to show rainfall, hail, and snow. Thunderstorms and lightning strikes can be added to the block through additional piecing, stitching, or embellishment. Whilst the temperature is the constant, those who make these textile records are free to interpret them in any way they choose.

On the 23rd March 2020, a few days prior to my encounter with Jo's temperature quilt blocks, British Prime Minster Boris Johnson announced measures to help stop the spread of COVID-19, including a national lockdown that would affect the lives of millions of people. Homes could only be left for limited reasons; workers were asked to avoid commuting and to work from makeshift offices at home if they could; dining tables became desks; non-essential shops were told to close. For everyone, the world suddenly became a lot smaller.

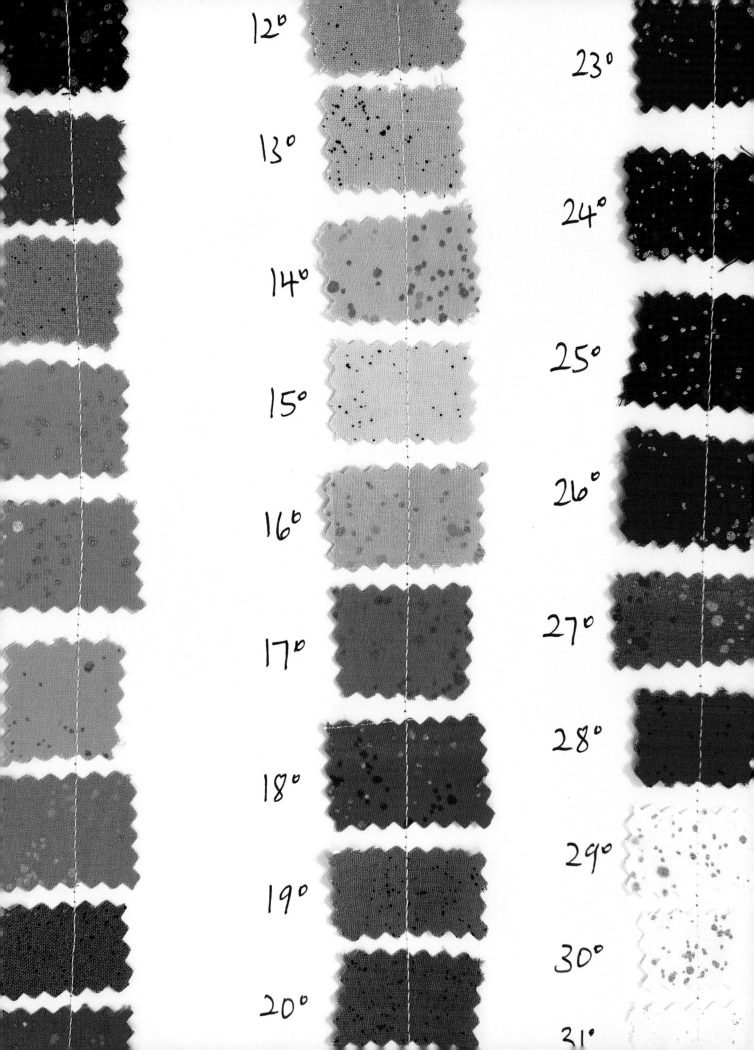

12°

13°

14°

15°

16°

17°

18°

19°

20°

23°

24°

25°

26°

27°

28°

29°

30°

31°

Faced with an unspecified period of isolation, I needed something to which I could dedicate my time; something that would occupy my mind and provide each day with a few brief moments of escapism. A temperature quilt seemed like the perfect answer. As if by some cosmic intervention, I'd recently begun devouring 'The Art of Manipulating Fabric' by Colette Wolff, a book so teeming with ideas that I didn't hesitate in incorporating one of them into my quilt. Improvisational at heart, I wanted the blocks to be something unexpected, something that wasn't me. I was looking for a creative challenge and found that in appliqué. My quilts have always been pieced. Even when attempting to replicate something which doesn't naturally lend itself to piecing, like an asparagus spear, I enjoy the challenge of utilising seams and figuring out the puzzle. For my temperature quilt, I decided to use stuffed appliqué to bring a tactile quality to the blocks. After a little trial and error, I began on the 15th April 2020.

My range of fabric spans deep petrol blues to burnt oranges. I'm not a fan of the traditional letterbox red that suggests heat, so opted for shocking pink to represent the upper limits of Cardiff's climate. When the mercury rose above what I thought would be the height of the summertime temperatures, I sought out brilliant white fabrics to record this rare occurrence and represent my intense dislike of extreme heat.

As for the shapes, I wanted them to be organic. Some were spontaneous; simple extensions of my hand, drawn in the moment and dictated by my mood. Others came from found objects: stones, twigs, and leaves from dog walks in the park or strolls along the shore. I used letters of significance and birthdays. I drew around objects of familiarity and comfort, including my grandmother's pin jar, a board game piece, and a pair of scissors. I took an empty toilet roll and drew around it in a nod to the now somewhat comical shortage faced by many countries, as we settled into the new normal of lockdown. Some shapes were inspired by defining moments throughout the year, such as the election of America's first female, African American and Asian American Vice President. I asked others, who had in some way contributed to the quilt, to draw a shape: Jo Avery for the inspiration, Giuseppe Ribaudo for designing some of the fabric used, and my close friend Ben for always listening to me as I vocalised my thoughts throughout my writing process. I set few parameters for the shapes, only that they should be organic and have no perfectly straight edges. With that in mind, the contributors were free to draw their shape, however they chose. I am particularly fond of Ben's effort, which is the 16th September, whose shape represents the USA and is a nod to our shared enjoyment of naming all fifty States in as short a time as possible.

As I went from day to day, recording the temperature and stuffing the shapes, they seemed to take on a viral quality, as if what was happening across the globe was manifesting itself in this piece. I began to view them not as leaves and shells, but as viruses under a microscope which, when considered collectively, record not only the temperature, but also a year that no one will ever likely forget.

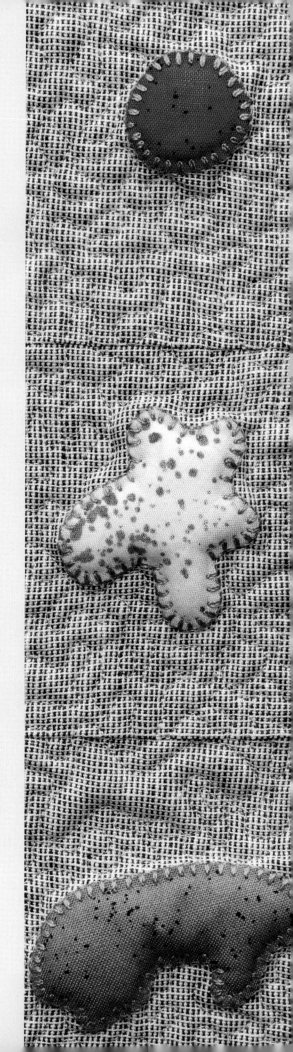

THE TECHNIQUE

STUFFED APPLIQUÉ

The trapunto technique is evident in some of the World's oldest quilts. One section of the Tristan quilt, made in Sicily during the latter part of the fourteenth century, is housed in London's Victoria and Albert Museum and depicts a select narrative of 'La Tavola Rotonada o L'Istoria di Tristano'. The design is stitched on linen and brought into relief through the insertion of cotton stuffing through the back. Great care was taken to part the fibres of the linen so that the stuffing could be passed through and evenly distributed. In trapunto quilts, the maker puts emphasis on the wadding, which is usually hidden, making it more important than simply a construction necessity.

Today, the handwork of this age-old technique has been all but replaced, as many quilters now use machine stitching to give the same effect. Designs are stitched through a fabric top and an initial layer of wadding using water soluble thread. The excess wadding is cut away before the piece is layered, with more wadding and backing fabric, then quilted to highlight the raised sections. Dense stitching around the trapunto design emphasises the technique and adds beautiful texture. Despite the option of a speedier machine method, the meditative process of stuffing each shape in the traditional way helped to focus my attention on something I could control, whilst distracting me from things I could not.

You can use any type of shape for this technique, large or small. They can be angular, or more organic like mine. Look for inspiration in nature or in the objects around you. I prefer to fuse my shapes into place using iron-on fusible web. Whilst this necessitates an extra step, I find I can more easily stitch the shape down when it is fully adhered to the background, rather than just pinned or tacked into position. Take care when stuffing the shapes, as too vigorous an effort can cause distortion or the stitching to break.

MATERIALS

Fabric scraps for the appliqué shapes

Larger pieces of background fabric, approximately ½" bigger than the required finished size of the block

Bondaweb or similar iron-on fusible fabric web

Lightweight tear-away stabiliser

Polyester fibre filling

Fray Check™ or similar

MAKING THE STUFFED APPLIQUÉ

1. Draw your shape onto the paper side of the iron-on fusible, ensuring that it is mirrored if the orientation is important; for example, when using a letter or number. Fuse to the wrong side of the shape fabric. *Fig a*

2. Cut out the shape, peel off the paper backing, and fuse to the right side of the background fabric, leaving excess fabric around the shape. This will ensure you have room to hoop the unit, as well as trim it down once it has been stuffed. *Figs b-d*

3. Before starting to sew, place a piece of stabiliser beneath the background fabric. Leave a long thread tail, then stitch the appliqué to the background fabric using either a straight, satin, or blanket stitch. Ensure that you use a stitch length small enough to prevent any open areas along the edge. For extra definition,

I used a heavier weight thread. Once the shape is stitched, leave another thread tail and remove it from the machine. Thread both top thread tails onto a hand sewing needle and pass through to the back. Secure with a knot and trim close to the surface of the background fabric. Repeat for the bobbin threads. Carefully remove the stabiliser from outside and inside the stitching line. Despite the tear-away nature of the stabiliser, I prefer to use sharp embroidery scissors for this and make small cuts close to the stitching. Take your time to avoid accidentally clipping the stitches. *Figs e-g*

4. Reactivate the adhesive of the fusible web by pressing with an iron for a couple of seconds. Before the piece cools, use a pin to pierce through the fibres behind the shape and separate the appliqué fabric from the

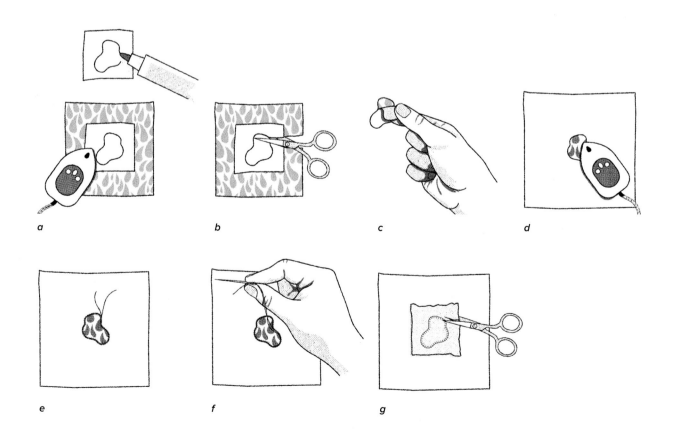

a

b

c

d

e

f

g

background fabric. Make small, sweeping motions with the length of a pin to unstick the fabrics. Once the layers are separated, cut a small slit across the bias of the background fabric at a central point inside the stitched perimeter of the shape. Depending on the shape, you may need to make more than one of these openings. Cutting across the bias helps to prevent the fabric from fraying too much when the shape is stuffed. *Figs h-i*

5. Insert the tip of a pair of long, slender tweezers in the slit and carefully push toward the stitched line, ensuring that all the fabric of the shape is free from the background fabric.

6. Place the unit into an embroidery hoop and use tweezers to stuff the shape. Prepare the fibre filling by "shredding" it through your fingers a few times to ensure a consistent texture. Aim to distribute the stuffing evenly by first pushing towards the stitched perimeter and filling any corners and angles.

Use wisps of stuffing for small sections, always working towards the centre. Check the front of the work frequently, to ensure even distribution of the filling. Take care not to over-stuff. You want the shape to be elevated, but not to a point where the stitching and surrounding fabric become distorted. *Figs j-l*

7. Thread a hand sewing needle with a finer weight thread and stitch the opening closed using an overcast stitch. Secure the stitching with a double knot and trim. *Figs m-n*

8. Apply a few drops of Fray Check or similar to the closed opening and allow to dry.

9. Remove the unit from the hoop and place it on a wool pressing mat. Carefully press from the back for a few seconds.

10. Trim the stuffed unit to the size required for your project. Refer to page 131 to see how I adapted a patchwork ruler to make this step easier.

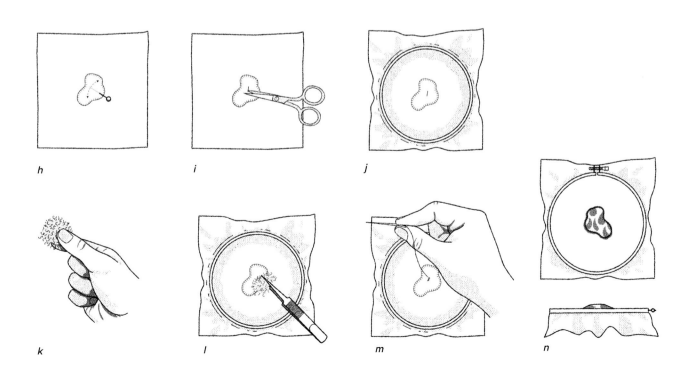

h

i

j

k

l

m

n

QUILTING NOTES

Everything about this quilt has been carefully chosen to draw attention to the appliqué shapes. It was important that the quilting did not distract, but highlight. A double layer of wadding (a cotton-poly blend beneath wool) helps to emphasise the trapunto effect, densely stitched down with micro stippling using a finer weight thread to blend into the background. This mesh of stitches flattens the wadding surrounding the shapes and helps disguise the seams of the joined units. Dense quilting will always elevate areas that are not quilted, so is a good choice when you want to draw the viewer's eye to a particular part of your design. Although a labour of love, the fruits of such labour are well worth the effort.

To highlight the dates on which it rained, hailed, or snowed, as well as when a lightning storm occurred, concentric rings have been quilted amongst the meandering stipple. One ring indicates rain, two hail, three snow, and four lightning. These organic shapes were not thought of in advance, but rather were stitched spontaneously by Trudi, mirroring the liberated nature of the appliqué.

LAYERED STUFFED APPLIQUÉ

The technique on pages 198 - 199 can be modified slightly to create layered appliqués where the shapes are stitched on top of each other in graduated sizes. Through experimentation, I've found that three to four layers are the most that can be stuffed before the shapes begin to distort.

First, draw your individual shapes onto the paper side of the iron-on fusible, ensuring that they nest on top of each other, with sufficient space around each layered shape for stuffing. Fuse onto the wrong side of the appliqué fabric and cut out. Before removing the paper and fusing the shapes, take the topmost shape, position it on the middle shape and draw a line 1/8" inch inside the perimeter. Using sharp embroidery scissors, carefully snip the centre of this drawn shape and cut it out, leaving a hole a little smaller than the shape you drew around. Repeat this process to draw around and cut out the middle shape on the bottom shape. By removing the excess fabric, not only is the bulk reduced, but you will now have access through the background fabric to stuff the pieces individually, once they are stitched down.

Starting with the bottom shape, remove the paper backing and fuse it to the background fabric. Position the middle shape over the cutout and fuse. Repeat for the topmost shape. Stitch each of the appliqués as in step 3, page 198, and then follow the rest of the steps to stuff them, beginning with the topmost shape.

A QUILT THAT CELEBRATES TRADITION

Hiraeth

BEHIND THE SEAMS

As I write this, the sun is slowly rising over Cardigan Bay on the West coast of Wales. A gossamer mist hangs above the surface of the distant water, soon to be burnt away as the mercury creeps towards uncomfortable highs. In the fields beyond, sheep serenade each other with shrieks and elongated bleating; sounds which are both eerie and comfortingly familiar.

This idyllic image of coast and countryside conjures up a version
of Wales familiar to many. Unchanged for centuries, Welshman
have used the land for housing, food, work, and play. The thriving
woollen industry of the nineteenth century, discussed previously,
was beneficial to the farmers who called this part of the country
home. Their flocks provided fleeces to the many woollen mills dotted
along the course of the River Teifi. These fleeces were processed and
painstakingly turned into flannel fabric, that then was as ubiquitous in
Wales as the green pastures and sheep that grazed them.

The Montgomeryshire ballad writer, George Thomas, lived through this industrial boom and describes the fabric's production process in this excerpt from his 1830 poem 'Welsh Flannel'.

First in his place, with keen attentive eyes,

To part the fleece the patient sorter plies;

The picker next makes clean each mossy lock,

The pitch cuts off that mark'd the shepherd's flock;

Soon thro' the willow's fangs the fleece is sent,

Here oil'd and toz'd in countless pieces rent:

Next thro' the scribbler's teeth must pass the whole,

And then the carder forms the perfect roll;

The piecer then exerts his infant skill

To join the rolls, and feed the slubbing bill;

The rolls half twisted by the slubber's art,

The skilful spinner next performs his part.

He little thinks, while round each spindle plays,

How soon his threads would compass earth and seas;

Nor does he think amidst the busy crowd,

Those self-same threads perchance may form his shroud.

The winder next in order does appear,

And then the warper forms the lengthen'd beer;

The warp in loom, and strengthen'd well with size,

Quick thro' its folds the weaver's shuttle flies.

The Flannel wove, the motes are pluck'd away,

And then 'tis cleans'd with soap and Fuller's clay;

Though no one seems to know for sure, the word flannel is believed to have derived from 'gwanlen', stemming from 'gwlan', the Welsh for wool. As well as being made into shirts, shawls, bedclothes, and underwear, we know that Welsh flannel found its way into countless quilts. One of the few remaining places that still produces and sells genuine Welsh wool flannel is Melin Teifi, a small and unassuming building tucked alongside the National Wool Museum in the village of Dre-fach Felindre. With a staff of eight, the workforce today is small compared to the many hundreds once employed by the thriving woollen industry. Inside the mill, a treasure trove awaits discovery by eager sewers. Rolls upon rolls of wool flannel are stacked towards the ceiling; traditional rich reds and deep blacks alongside more muted creams and whites.

Many of today's quilters are overly familiar with cotton and use this fabric staple exclusively in their quilt making. The wide range of prints, availability, and ease of use make cotton the most popular choice for patchwork. Yet, using different textiles in our quilts brings new and exciting textures. I wanted to use Welsh flannel not only to add a tactile element, but also as a way of celebrating past makers and an important part of Welsh history. By using this homegrown fabric, I felt a connection to my forebears, whose extensive use of wool flannel would have been much more utilitarian than my own.

The importance of this fabric to Wales was reiterated by George Thomas, who went on to say:

Man owes a double debt to Flannel white,

His vest by day, his blanket warm by night.

The prop of life in each succeeding stage;

The nurse of youth, and comforter of age;

His first best garb when hurri'd from the womb,

And his last robe, to shroud him in the tomb.

To make this quilt, I stripped myself of my modern quilter trappings and used scissors to cut and shape the flannel. As would have been done traditionally, I pieced a central block, to which I added successive borders and quarter-square triangles. The flannel is paired with shot cotton to add both tactile and visual contrast.

The title of this quilt is not one easily translated. Sometimes language can fall short when describing things that are felt. 'Hiraeth' cannot be conveyed in a single English word. It is multi-layered, emotive, and suggests longing, homesickness, or deep yearning for the past. It can also suggest grief for people or places lost. In this context, the quilt is so-called to describe my nostalgia for Wales, and the way the Country once was.

41" X 39"

THE TECHNIQUE

BIG STITCH HAND QUILTING

These are not the pages for a comprehensive tutorial and whilst I am by no means an authority on hand quilting, there are nonetheless some techniques that work well for me, when taking this more liberated approach. If you have not quilted in this way before, I encourage you to experiment to find a way of stitching that works best for you.

• With traditional hand quilting, there is an emphasis placed on the importance of a consistent stitch length, with smaller stitches often being considered "better". The stitches seen in antique Welsh quilts range from ten to fourteen per inch. As you develop your hand quilting skills, you'll be able to make smaller stitches. For big stitch quilting, especially if a thicker thread is being used, the stitches should be larger and bold, with uniformity not so important.

• The use of a hoop or frame will add support to the quilt sandwich, however, whether they are more convenient or cumbersome is often debated by quilters. I prefer to stitch without a hoop, instead laying the quilt layers over a table for extra support.

• Finding the right tools for the job inevitably involves some trial and error. Needles come in various types and sizes, so what works for one quilter may not be the best choice for you. I prefer a longer, finer needle that has a little give and allows me to load the needle with more stitches.

• With big stitch quilting, rather than rocking the needle and loading stitches onto it, I sometimes use a stabbing method. I pass the needle down vertically through the fabric, then use my other hand placed under the quilt to pull it through a little way, before stabbing it back through further along the stitching line. I find this works well for smaller, tighter circles, ovals, and swirls.

QUILTING NOTES

Whilst I didn't go as far as to hand piece the quilt, I did hand quilt it. This was the first time I'd used hand quilting and whilst my calloused fingertips would vehemently disagree, I thoroughly enjoyed the process. I felt a real connection to those Welsh quilters that came before me, who would have stood at the quilting frame and sectioned off areas of fabric with chalked string. For the quilters of nineteenth century Wales, their craft would have been a way of earning money, rather than a leisure activity. By stitching in this way, I enhanced my understanding of these time-honoured techniques.

The quilting seen on traditional Welsh wholecloth and flannel quilts is among the best in the world. I wanted my quilting to be a little more defined than what would traditionally be used on a Welsh quilt. Using a heavier weight wool thread and the folksier look of big stitches, I chose to quilt in a broad way, using the piecing as a framework for the designs. Alongside rows of stitching, I used traditional Welsh motifs such as hearts, leaves, and pears. As many quilters would have done, I utilised common household items, such as plates, pastry cutters, and lids to mark the stitching lines in chalk. The design was loosely planned beforehand, allowing the work to shift and change as the quilting progressed.

WELSH BUTTED EDGE

After completing the quilting, my research led me to discover a traditional way of finishing this quilt. Rather than being bound or faced, Welsh quilts used a butted or knifed edge to secure the raw edges. Thinking back, I remembered observing how the flannel quilts at the Unforgettable exhibition at the Welsh Quilt Centre had no visible edge finishing. I had assumed they were faced, yet now believe they were completed in this new-to-me way.

Use a Welsh butted edge as an alternative to the more common edge finishing techniques. It is particularly suited to quilts where the quilting does not go right to the perimeter. A good 2" will give you the space needed to turn back the quilt edge. Additional quilting can then be added after the edge is sewn.

FINISHING THE QUILT EDGE

1. After quilting, trim the excess backing and wadding level with the quilt top. *Fig a*

2. Fold back the quilt top and backing and trim the wadding by approximately ½", taking care not to cut into the top or bottom fabric. *Fig b*

3. Fold the excess backing down on top of the wadding, then fold the excess top fabric in, so that the fold meets the folded edge of the backing fabric. *Fig c*

4. Using a matching thread, stitch a small running stitch as close to the folded edge as you can. To secure and change thread, tie a knot close to the surface of the quilt, insert the needle through the quilt top and wadding only, come out a few inches away and tug the knot though into the middle of the quilt. Trim the thread tail. *Fig d*

5. To finish the corners, first stop stitching 4" to 6" away. This is important as you need the space to fold the fabric. Stitching too close to the corner will make it more difficult. On the quilt top, fold down the top edge first, then the side. On the quilt back, do the opposite. First fold the side in to meet the wadding, then the top. The resulting folds can then be butted together neatly and stitched in place. *Figs e-g*

6. Continue stitching and folding until all the quilt edge is turned in. An optional second line of stitching can be quilted ¼" away from the first. *Fig h*

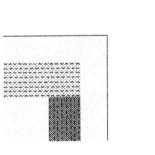

a

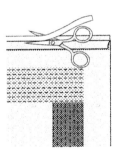

b

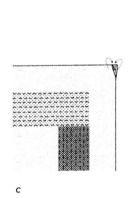

c

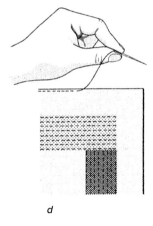

d

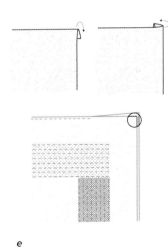

e

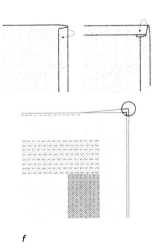

f

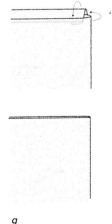

g

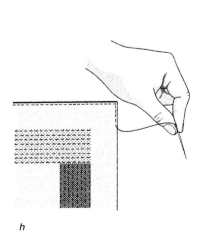

h

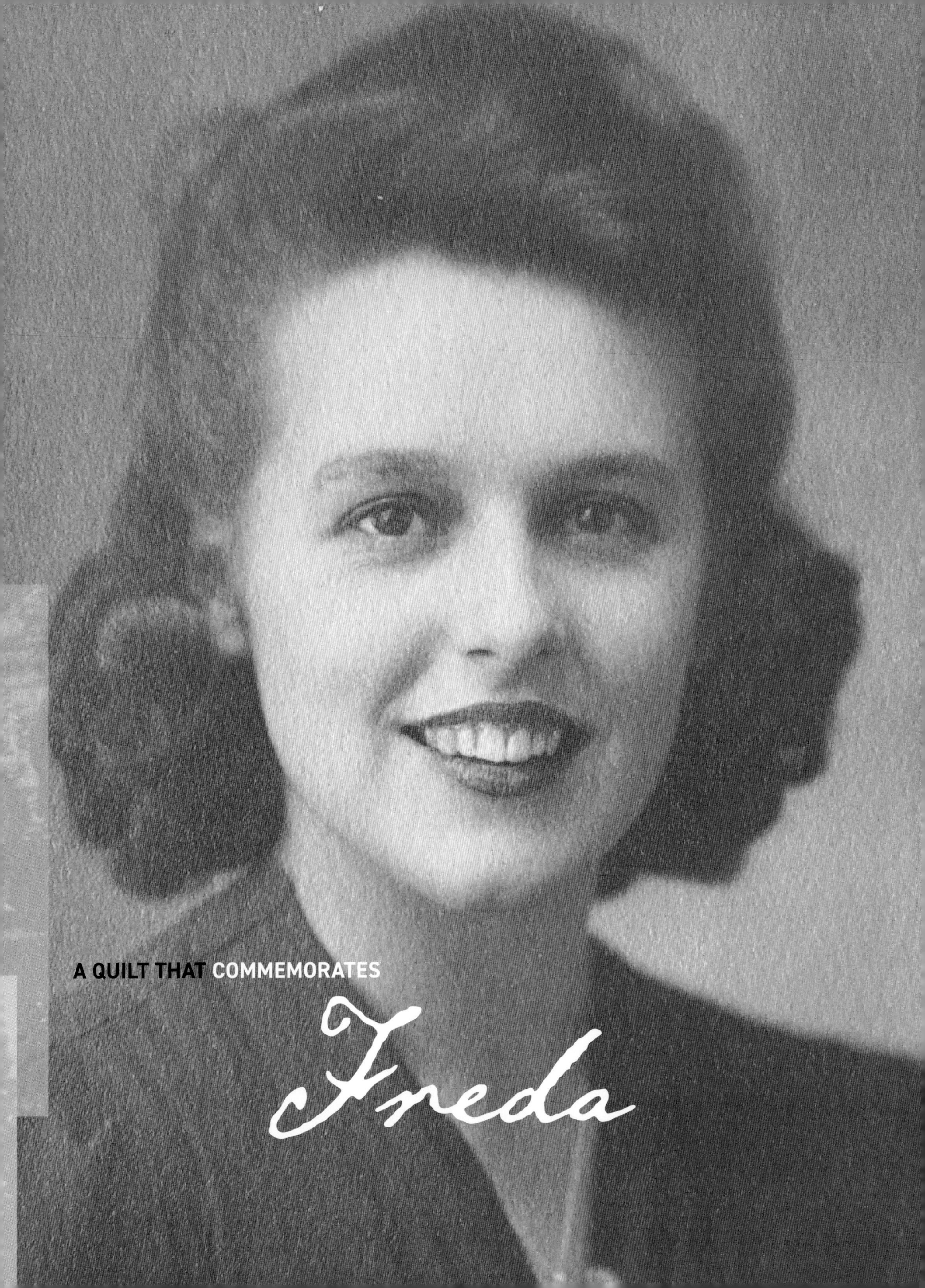

A QUILT THAT COMMEMORATES

Freda

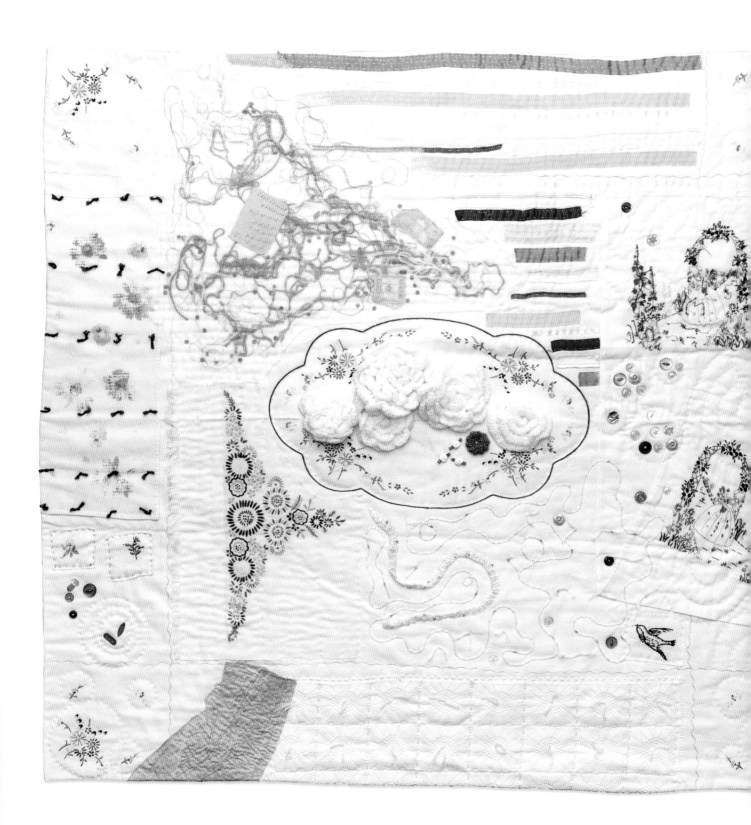

43" X 39"

BEHIND THE SEAMS

As I mentioned in this book's introduction, there is not a rich quilting history in my family. As much as I'd love to say that my ancestors were avid quilters, the truth is I know of few family members who expressed any form of creativity. My father's trade was wood. As a child I remember being fascinated by the possibilities of the offcuts he gave me to experiment with. The smell of sawdust and wood glue still evoke memories of the makeshift houses and crude cars that I enthusiastically built. I'd spend hours thumbing through each new edition of the 'Hobbies' catalogue and marvel at the assortment of toy patterns and dollhouse plans. To my naive perception of time, the wait for delivery after my father bought one was agonisingly long, this being pre-home internet and the downloadable PDF.

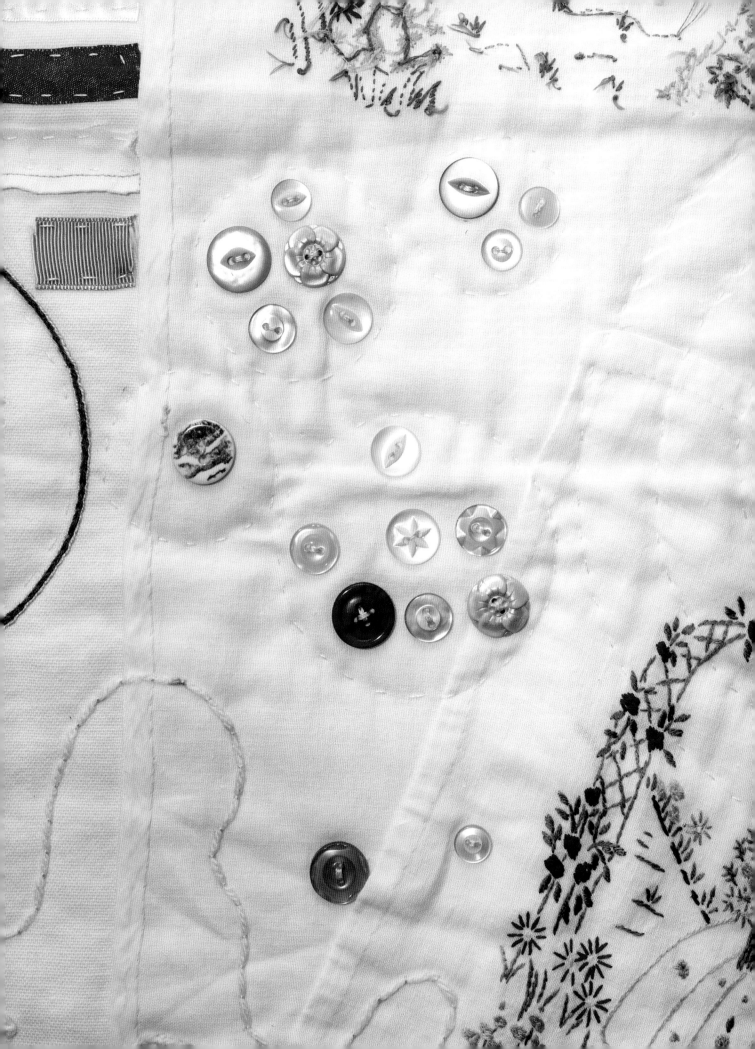

My most endearing memories of creativity are focused sharply around my grandmother. It's almost impossible for me to not recall some childhood memory of sewing or baking with her whenever I partake in these activities today. She taught me how to plant bulbs and weed flower beds; how to draw using simple shapes; how to make dumplings, fruit cakes, and gravy. We completed countless cross stitch kits together, pressed flowers between pieces of corrugated cardboard and, with much patience and perseverance, she taught me how to knit garter stitch, the only knitting I could grasp at the time.

Freda Winifred Edith Ball had all the stereotypical qualities of the warm and kindly grandmother. She spoke with remarkable candour about her past experiences: life during the Second World War, rationing, and raising three children after the premature death of my grandfather in 1959. She knitted, baked avidly, and loved flowers. Her home was full of trinkets and teapots, each object fascinating to my young eyes. There were brass candlesticks which she showed me how to polish using the big tin of Brasso under the sink; an L.S Lowry print hung on the back bedroom wall; a ceramic fruit bowl with a chip in one of the leaves. Yet most alluring was her sewing box; a somewhat tatty, woven thing brimming with needles, pins, and threads, as well as a curious pair of scissors I now know to be pinking shears. Through slip knots and stitch, she passed on her passion for craft to me. After she passed away in 2019 at the impressive age of ninety-one, this sewing box, along with her knitting bag and embroideries, came to me. I'd seen many examples of memory quilts that featured clothing, so I wanted to do something similar to showcase Freda's handiwork. I stored these possessions for almost two years before carefully considering the best way to incorporate them into a quilt.

Freda is my homage to my grandmother and the many leisurely pursuits she enjoyed. It began with an idea for an improvised appliqué. I wanted to use the embroidery pieces in such a way so as to showcase their simplicity and delicateness. I decided against patchwork, instead using a whole tablecloth as a background for further embellishment. The quilt evolved as I discovered the contents of the sewing box. Smaller examples of embroidery were quilted down. I used a hammer to extract the dye from the garden's summer bedding plants and pattern some table linen with imprints of the flowers she so loved. I embellished with strips of ribbon and hand-tied sections of the quilt using wool wound into balls by her hand. From her knitting needles, I carefully removed the last stitches she cast on and stitched them to the foundation, couching down the remaining yarn to meet the beak of an embroidered bird. Robins were her favourite, so I added a red breast to one of her outlined birds. A stitched collaboration which spans decades.

Throughout the construction of this quilt, Freda watched from her vantage point on my notice board. A picture I took of us both stirred my brain in the same way that the embroideries did as they moved beneath my fingertips. The smell of my grandmother's house rose up from the cotton fabric; her wool evoked olfactory memories of casting on and failing at purl stitch; her not-so-well-formed handwriting on scraps of paper transporting me back to spellings tests, crosswords, and a yellowing notebook in which recipes were jotted down. Making this quilt was emotional. I like to think that in every quilt I make, I stitch a little of myself into it. It's comforting to know that in this one, I have company.

THE TECHNIQUE

LAYERING

Within the stained lining of the sewing box, I found many treasures: hand-wound skeins of embroidery floss, wooden spools of thread, sequins, snap fastener packaging, a few tiny pieces from the felt board of my childhood, and a precious scrap of cardboard marked by grandmother's hand with the carefully counted rows of a knitting project. Inspired by Heidi Parkes, I carefully unravelled the threads and layered them with the other items before covering the assortment of lines and shapes with a fine muslin. I quilted through the layers to preserve those things which my grandmother had touched.

This technique would work equally well with scraps of fabric, perhaps trimmings from a favourite quilt or a confetti of smaller pieces not quite big enough to piece together. You can either layer the pieces to a block and sew those blocks together, or use a wholecloth approach as I did, and layer sections.

MATERIALS

Oddments of yarn, embroidery thread, sequins, or small fabric trimmings

A foundation fabric, either cut to size for a block or a larger background piece for a wholecloth quilt

Fine muslin or silk scrim

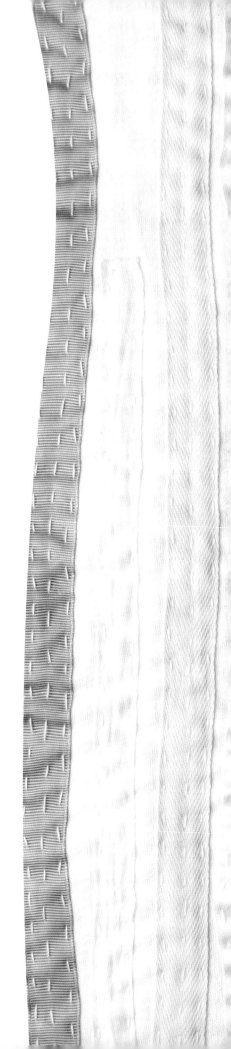

QUILTING NOTES

Other than the facing, there is no machine stitching on this quilt. I chose to use hand quilting to complement my grandmother's embroideries. Some sections have curved shapes echo quilted through the layers. Some of the embroidery motifs are highlighted by rings of stitches. I used a dense pattern of random stitches to secure a scrap of the sewing box's lining to the tablecloth background. As well as using her embroidery floss, I used oddments of her yarn to tie sections of the quilt together.

CREATING THE LAYERING

1. Layer the fabric trimmings, yarn, threads, or ribbons onto the foundation fabric. You can take time to place them or allow them to fall in a more random arrangement. *Fig a*

2. Carefully lay a piece of muslin over the arrangement, ensuring that it is big enough to cover all the pieces you have positioned.

3. Using a contrasting, fine weight thread, baste the edge of the muslin into place, keeping the foundation fabric flat so as not to disturb the loose pieces beneath the muslin. *Fig b*

4. Once basted into position, trim away the excess and quilt through the muslin and foundation fabric. I used big stitches and a heavier weight thread. Be sure to quilt densely enough so that the loose pieces are held in place. Remove the basting stitches if desired. *Fig c*

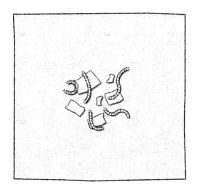

a

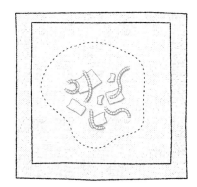

b

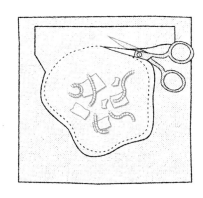

c

QUILTING **COLLABORATIONS**

Despite social media and the daily interactions I have with quilters around the world, quilting for me is a solitary activity. I am alone in my sewing room, working on a piece that has been envisaged, designed, and constructed solely by me. I briefly explored the idea of collaboration during my early foray into quilting through participation in bees and block swaps. This not only provided me with the opportunity of meeting fellow quilters, but also presented a creative challenge of taking someone else's work and unifying it with my own.

These days, collaboration comes in the form of working with a long-arm quilter. Years ago, I was surprised to hear of quilters who loved to piece their tops, yet dreaded the act of quilting the layers together. The size of their ambition, coupled with the narrow throat of their sewing machines, resulted in a war of push and pull with which I could empathise. Wrestling large amounts of fabric and wadding under a small sewing machine is no easy feat, and I knew too well the heartbreak of turning a quilt over and seeing the back marred with pleats and tucks. I soon discovered the existence of people who would gladly take your tops and quilt them for you. I was intrigued.

I remember the first time I saw a long-arm machine. My first thought was "*look at all the space*"; the idea of being able to have the full width of a quilt top laid out in front of me, taut and ready to quilt, was so appealing. I was enamoured with the amazing designs stitched out by these machines that moved on a frame whilst the quilt layers remained stationary. Some were long, industrial-looking machines, whilst others looked much like my sewing machine, albeit attached to a set of wheels. Trudi Wood, a long-arm quilter from Lincoln, UK, not only gave me my first glimpse into the life of a long-armer, but has become a close friend and the only other person who has quilted my work. Trudi has been quilting for over thirty years. For her, it was the serendipitous discovery of a quilting catalogue that ignited a spark for patchwork. Having studied engineering and drawing, the geometry of traditional piecing was immediately appealing. Though now a master of free motion, her very first quilt was hand quilted.

"Back in the late eighties and early nineties it was a heinous crime to machine quilt. However, there were people like Linda Taylor, Sharon Schamber, and Sue Patton who were the big girls, the pioneers of machine quilting. I always wanted to do what the big girls did, so I taught myself to quilt using a machine."

In 2007, after many years of quilting by moving the fabric, Trudi purchased a tabletop frame to house her domestic sewing machine and allow her the functionality of a long-arm. She used her straight-stitch Juki for its speed and learnt the movement and design of long-arm free-motion quilting. In 2014, her long-arm frame machine arrived from the USA and she has been custom quilting for clients ever since. I remember Trudi sharing progress of the frame's assembly on her Instagram. Her excitement was infectious.

"To go from a nine-inch harp to a twenty-two-inch harp machine was like, wow, I can do really big designs! For me, the transition from domestic sewing machine to long-arm was about learning to work in these new parameters. Because I was well-versed in free motion movement, I had to master the space, rather than the machine."

My quilting collaborations with Trudi span nine-odd years. We first met face-to-face during a quilting retreat in July 2014. It was at this retreat where I met Jo Avery and discovered Aurifil thread, so a moment of many fortuitous firsts! I had taken a free motion quilting class with Trudi and afterwards we began sharing ideas for finishing the quilt I was making. Inspired by the

spines of Penguin Classics paperbacks, I wanted the quilting to add texture and suggest wear and age. Now knowing her reputation for quilting elaborate feathers and swirls, asking Trudi to stitch straight lines over and over again was a little like asking Picasso to paint your kitchen ceiling. Yet she graciously accepted, and so began a wonderfully inspiring and creative relationship.

When working together on a piece, the process often begins with Trudi and I discussing what the quilt represents. Different from a traditional quilt, where Trudi may quilt a design in a block, add some backfill, and finish with a border, an improv quilt, with its lack of visible block structure and irregular edges, requires a different conversation. Through these conversations, we cultivate an understanding of our ways of working and build a personal connection which is as important as our connection to the quilt. Ideas are bounced back and forth, with Trudi suggesting things I may not have considered. She'll often print images of the quilt top and doodle away suggestions of lines and shapes. There is a familiarity and an understanding now. Trudi knows to expect wavy edges and non-square quilts from me. If I'm able to give her one straight edge or seam, all the better. I've learnt that stay-stitching the edges of my quilt tops makes her life easier too. Inspirational photographs are exchanged, thread colour is discussed, and a plan slowly comes together.

"We talk through ideas. Sometimes you agree and say you like the idea. Other times you feel that an idea is good but it's not right for this quilt."

Since the Penguin Classics quilt, our collaborations have transitioned to a more organic place and have produced quilts that I am immensely proud of. Among the three featured in 'Inspiring Improv', most notable was How to Age a Tree. I have talked at length about my experience of making that quilt and the way it challenged and shaped me as a quilter. The afterword of 'Inspiring Improv' details how I asked Trudi to cut the quilt in half to avoid a nightmarish situation of having to re-make it from scratch. She recalls the moment I made the request.

"I was quite shocked. I've been asked to do many things to a quilt, but never to cut one in half. I was absolutely petrified of ruining it. I actually cried, because there was so much in that act of cutting and I value our friendship. Quite frankly, to do all that work again if you didn't like how I'd cut it...I felt sick! I take my hat off to Victoria Findlay Wolfe, who too has cut up a whole pieced quilt. Yet, as with the tree quilt, doing so made it something so much more than what it was before."

Trudi was pleased to hear that there would be no further cutting of quilts for our latest collaborations. I'm am honoured that she has once again become part of the story of four quilts featured in this book. With my favourite firmly decided, I was interested to hear her thoughts on quilting these pieces.

"They were all very different. The fish quilt allowed me to be really creative. It was just a case of going for it, with lots of chalk marking for reference. I loved the whole journey of the black and white quilt. At the start of the process, I had ideas and that was one quilt where you decided to stick with your original plan. I have to honour your decision because that clearly made such a difference. The whole journey the quilt takes you on, its meaning, was very moving."

Cheshire Puss is another example of the benefits of collaboration. I had originally decided upon echo quilting within each letter, yet Trudi was of a mind that the quilt didn't need it. After quilting a small section, she sent an image that showed she was right.

"What you always bring to your quilts is a love of dense quilting. The background of that quilt is so dense, the letters just stand out and speak for themselves. Thread colour was very a much key. The pink we used tones down some of the brighter fabrics, but brings up the lighter, less saturated ones. You have a more even colour spread because of the choice of thread."

After a traditionally pieced quilt top is quilted, although the edges are yet to be trimmed and bound, the final size and shape of the quilt is evident at that point. My work, even at that late stage, is still evolving. With a quilt like Cheshire Puss, I often have to trim some of the quilted top away to create the edges I need. For this reason, the boundaries of my quilts are often oversized. Trudi quilts the areas regardless, knowing that some of her work will be lost. When trimming I refer to these pieces as casualties, yet she doesn't see it that way, describing the trimming as *"part of a no-boundaries process".*

Of all the quilts we have worked on, Viral Temperature is my favourite. Trudi has put more of herself into this quilt than in any of our other collaborations. During its construction, we had long conversations about the best way to make the appliqués stand out even more. Trudi agrees that it was a challenge.

"We explored lots of wadding options. I created samples of different wadding combinations and density of stitching. Double wadding was key and when I began to quilt, I was surprised at just how much the appliqués puffed up thanks to the dense stipple, which I nearly went blind from! I could only quilt in small bursts, half an hour at a time, due to the strain on my eyes. I learnt something new from that quilt: magnifying glasses help! What I love about that quilt is that so many other people were involved, not just you and I. It means so many things to so many people. I was given free rein to do the weather quilting. I have never received a quilt with a postcard reference before! The quilt was covered with safety pins and scraps, and I had to work through and reference that key. I love the texture of it, the depth of the appliqués. It blows my mind what we've achieved. You had a clear image of how you wanted it to look and we've done that."

AFTERWORD:
Red Carpet Recognition

On the 13th September 2021, photographers stood poised outside New York's Metropolitan Museum of Art, ready to capture the attendees at the Met Gala. This now world-famous event has a colourful history, first conceived in 1948 as a charity function to raise money for the newly founded Costume Institute. Since the early seventies, the Met Gala has marked the opening of the Institute's annual exhibition and has become synonymous with high fashion and lavish costuming, its themes encompassing a broad spectrum, from the fantastical to the politically charged. Each year, celebrities from film, music, and the arts grace the red carpet, their couture carefully considered to match the exhibition concept. The garments ooze drama. They are widely photographed and critiqued, often influencing fashion retailers for many months after.

The first of a two-part exhibition, In America: A Lexicon of Fashion, opened on the 18th September 2021 and took inspiration for its design from Adeline Harris Sears' Autograph quilt; a mid-nineteenth century piece in The Met's American Wing collection. The quilt, made from close to two thousand individually cut and sewn silk pieces signed by many celebrities of the day, formed the basis of the exhibition's installation, with display cases representing the patches of the quilt, each containing an example of American fashion history.

Patchwork is no stranger to the runway. Many designers have created sartorial collections that take inspiration from quilt blocks, handwork, and ideas of repurposing and make-do and mend. Emily Adams Bode's fall 2020 collection was an exploration of craft. Ronald van Der Kemp, well-known for his use of re-appropriated materials, showcased several garments in his 2019 fall couture collection. They evoked the crazy quilts of the Victorian era, lavishly embellished with hand embroidery and decorative stitching.

At the 2021 Met Gala, patchwork was once again thrust onto the global stage. Anna Wintour, Editor-in-Chief of 'Vogue' and chairwoman of the Gala, said of the theme "*American fashion is a celebration of exuberance, joy, and creativity...what it has become in 2021 is a patchwork, reflecting the world we're all living in...*". As guests entered the museum and cameras flashed, a look appeared that perfectly captured the essence of Americana. The rapper A$AP Rocky arrived last with the singer and actress Rihanna; she in a ruffled and voluminous black Balenciaga overcoat, he in a tuxedo layered beneath a bright and whimsical quilt. Years before it was repurposed for the red carpet by designer Eli Russell Linnetz, the puff quilt Rocky was enveloped in had been donated to a thrift store. Now, in a stunning revival, it was reimagined in a creative collaboration with Zak Foster. In an interview not long after the event, Zak talked about the early ideas put forward by Eli. The original plan was to re-make the vintage quilt. But owing to time constraints, this was abandoned in favour of attaching a new quilt

forming the other side, taking the place of the plain grey backing. Zak pieced a second quilt from vintage plaids and flannels and hand-tied it to the original, preserving all of its memories. Zak's contribution was revealed in dramatic fashion as A$AP Rocky disrobed, exposing the vibrancy and vitality of the red fabric.

Viewing quilts as art is a modern notion. The idea of signing their work was not something considered by early quilters, so many antique quilts remain unattributed. The original maker of the puff quilt might have forever remained unknown, if not for social media. In a warming postscript to the story, the quilt was recognised by the great granddaughter of the original maker, who remembered it lying atop her old bed before it was donated. How warming to think that this quilter's work now lives on. It has become part of a bigger, multi-character story. From humble beginnings, it now occupies a space that defies definition and has been elevated to a position that blurs the lines of what a quilt is and can be.

ACKNOWLEDGEMENTS

I didn't think I would write another book. I was too afraid of encountering that second album syndrome musicians talk about, especially since this effort entwines techniques and tips with history and fact. The words were no longer solely about me and my quilting. There is no denying that it was a unique challenge, during which I frequently questioned my ability and credentials to achieve. I was roused from periods of doubt by friends and family, and supported through the long process by the quilting community for whom I have so much admiration.

Barri and Samuel: you have to exist on the periphery of this quilting world in which I have set up camp. It encroaches on your lives in subtle ways and pulls me away from family time, yet you are always supportive and allow me to get on with things.

Mother and Father: thank you for your continued support. I did mention that this quilting thing was here to stay.

Grandmother: you never got to hold 'Inspiring Improv' in your hands, but know that everything that has come since, has a little of you in it. Thank you for your embroideries and the contents of your sewing box. Placing my stitches alongside yours was so comforting. I hope you like our collaboration. I miss you.

Bruce: your faith and unwavering support made writing this book easier. Thank you for allowing me to express myself without constraint and to contribute to the continuing Lucky Spool tradition. I know that Susanne would be proud.

Trudi: I finished acknowledging you in 'Inspiring Improv' with the words "*here's to many more collaborations*". I cannot thank you enough for instilling my quilts with your talent, passion, and love. The Viral Temperature quilt making the cover of this book shows the wonderful things that happen when you become part of the story of my quilts.

Jen Jones: the quilts of Wales are indebted to your dedication. Thank you for being so generous with your time and knowledge.

Hazel: thank you for your assistance and for providing images of Jen's quilts.

To the staff at the National Wool Museum: it was wonderful of you to accommodate us and allow photography of my flannel quilt in a very special location. Thank you.

The past and present quilters of Gee's Bend: I know I speak for countless quilters when I say you are truly inspirational.

Jo, Russell, Jen, Chris, Tara, Zak, Luke, Debbie, Heidi, Drew, and Melanie: thank you so much for being a part of this book. You are all wonderfully kind and generous with your time. Your work is truly inspiring and I'm so pleased I got to share it. Many of my own quilts featured in this book were inspired by you.

Mark and El: as far as photography goes, it's not always easy for me to take a back seat, though I think it's safe to say it paid off. Thank you for your hard work and creative approach. You have showcased these quilts exceptionally well and in doing so, I'm glad you got the opportunity to explore Wales. I can only apologise for the lack of rain!

Ian: once again you have taken my haphazard sketches and rushed samples to create illustrations that clearly show my techniques. Thank you for being so good at what you do.

Megan: it was a joy to work with you on this book. You have produced something truly beautiful. Thank you.

Nydia: our streams of messages are testimony to the love and support you provide, especially during the moments of heightened stress that come with writing a book. You often give me other, superior options, taking the work to new and exciting heights. I will never tire of brainstorming with you. Know that through your advice, my quilts have once again become all the better.

Ben: much appreciation for showing me the answer is there, even though it's not always the one I was looking for.

Melanie Reed: you generously helped me when fabric and time were running out. Thank you for sharing your sewalong story.

Sarah Ashford: thank you for encouragement and for rewarding my milestones with chocolate.

Bogod and Bernina UK: thank you for your continued support.

The quilts in this book were made with the support and generosity of the sewing and quilting community. I would like to extend my extreme gratitude to Aurifil, Barnyarns, Dashwood Studio, Hobbs, Lovely Jubbly Fabrics, Oakshott, and The Sewing Studio.

To anyone who has made an improv quilt: I thank you for being a part of a rich and captivating story whose chapters will continue to be written as new people become enamoured with this liberating way of quilting.